AF335227

The Mission of Santa Barbara in 1880

From an Etching by Henry Chapman Ford

THE EARLY DAYS

—OF—

SANTA BARBARA

CALIFORNIA

FROM THE FIRST DISCOVERIES BY
EUROPEANS TO DECEMBER, 1846

—BY—

WALTER A. HAWLEY

AUTHOR OF

"ORIENTAL RUGS"

AND

"ASIA MINOR"

ILLUSTRATED

REPRINT
Published by

James Stevenson Publisher
Fairfield, CA
james.stevenson@jspub.com

SANTA BARBARA

1920

March 2003 printing
of the Second (1920) Edition

The Early Days of Santa Barbara, California

ISBN 1-885852-37-1

Library of Congress Control Number 2003103499

Press of
The Schauer Printing Studio
Santa Barbara

PREFACE

IN DISREGARD of the historic value of the old buildings of the Mission, Presidio, and Pueblo of Santa Barbara—precious monuments sacred to the memory of men who will be remembered for generations to come—tiled roofs have been destroyed, walls allowed to crumble, and foundations effaced. Already some of the most interesting buildings have gone. Even their former locations are known to few.

Fifteen years ago, realizing how rapidly the old landmarks were dissappearing, the writer with the assistance of an engineer made surveys both at the Mission and at the presidio of all the buildings then standing, and also of all the ruins and traces of foundations of former buildings. These surveys were then carefully platted.

This work was done on account of a personal interest in the subject, and with the view of placing the data, thus obtained, at the disposal of any one competent and willing to write the history of the early days of Santa Barbara. But the subject has awakened but little interest in the historian; and as some of the ruins that were then surveyed have since disappeared, the writer now offers this little sketch, accompanied by plans of the Mission and presidio, made from the original surveys, in the hope that it will create a greater interest in the lives and works of the founders of this beautiful city.

At the time of making the surveys, the writer consulted a number of the oldest residents, who are no longer living; and made notes regarding the old ruins and early history of Santa Barbara. He has also gathered facts from nearly every source, regarded as reliable; so that he is more or less indebted to nearly every writer on the early history of California, and particularly to the Rev. J. J. O'Keef and the Rev. Juan Caballeria.

SANTA BARBARA, *December* 20, 1909.

CONTENTS

ILLUSTRATIONS

FOREWORD

It is my privilege to answer the repeated requests of the public in republishing this book written by the late Walter A. Hawley.

It's worth is appreciated by the student for its accuracy as to date and detail of event. And to those minds of lighter vein it holds its own charm—permanently placing itself in the substantial chronicles of early California life.

R. C. H.

INTRODUCTORY

THE history of the early days of Santa Barbara not only awakens the general interest which is felt in the causes which lead to the founding of all cities and in the economic reasons for their subsequent growth, but also arouse a special interest, as this city is one of the few in the United States founded by an alien race. However excellent the traits and institutions of the Anglo-Saxon race may be, each of the other races which founded cities within the United States has contributed something to be admired. The towns of New York State founded by the Dutch have been influenced by the sterling qualities of that race; New Orleans still reflects the spirit of the French, both in its interesting architecture and the fascinating society; and the cities founded by the Spanish in Florida and the southwest have a fascination distinctly referable to their founders.

In the Mission style of architecture, characterizd by its strong yet simple lines, the Spanish introduced a style which probably has no superior in unaffected beauty. The Spanish have also contributed to the charm of social life in all cities which they founded.

The City of Santa Barbara is one of the best representatives of the cities of the southwest founded by the Spanish or their descendants. Its Mission Church is not only typical of that style of architecture, but is the best preserved of any in California. Also, as recorded by writers who visited this city three-quarters of a century ago, the society here was at that time more aristocratic and refined than on any other part of the coast; and the city still feels the influence of that early Spanish atmosphere which adds greatly to its interest. Accordingly, the study of the early history of this city and of the life of its founders should be particularly attractive.

Many of the earliest pioneers of California were not Spanish of pure blood, but Mexican descendants of Spaniards married to the natives of Mexico. The latter are far more capable and interesting than is generally known. At the time of the conquest of Cortez, the native races had advanced to a state of semi-civilization, To-day not only do they cultivate their own ranches, work their own mines, and engage in various lines of industry, but some of them are men of great force and ability. The present ruler of Mexico, who is one of the ablest of the living rulers, is a Mexican of nearly pure native blood. The natives are also artistic and musical; and many of those whose ancestors have for generations lived among the mountains of Mexico, remote from the refining influences of city life, show a charm of manner and delicacy of sentiment which are remarkable. To the descendants of these native races of Mexico, intermarrying with the Spaniards, is due the credit for the founding and building of the pueblos and Missions, and the picturesqueness of the early life of California.

THE ABORIGINES

IT WOULD be interesting, if it were possible, to see this part of the coast as it was a little over a century ago. There has been but little change in the natural scenery, but it was probably even more beautiful then than now. The rugged peaks and upper ridges of the Santa Ynez mountains were more heavily timbered with pine, and the valleys were more heavily wooded with oaks. The face of the land was neither plowed, nor fenced, nor disfigurd by artificial roads. In the spring of the year, the surface of every valley and rolling hill was covered with bright wild flowers; and in the fall, it was a matting of sun-browned grass and aromatic tarweed. The same ocean girded the coast with its chain of islands, and reflected a blue more beautiful than Italian skies. Nor was nature inanimate; as droves of deer rested in the shade of the woods, bear hid in recesses of the canyons, and otter sported in the kelp, while birds of varied plumage unmolested, claimed their natural homes.

But if there has been but little change in scenery, the change in many other respects is very marked. A city inhabited by enlightened and cultured people, now occupies the sloping plain which was then a broad field, dotted with groves of oaks and marked with lines of sycamores which followed the arroyo banks. In the lower stretches of the plain and in the neighboring valleys were Indian rancherias or villages. Over these hills and through these valleys the Indians roamed and hunted, and out in the channel they fished.

Compared with other races of American Indians, those of the Santa Barbara Channel would rank neither among the highest nor lowest in intellectual and social development. They showed nothing of that progress towards civilization which characterized the Incas of Peru and the Aztecs of Mexico; yet in many interesting particulars they showed marked superiority over the other tribes of this coast. The Santa Ynez and San Rafael ranges of mountains separated them so effectually from the races to the north and east, that they enjoyed almost constant immunity from hostile attack; a climate, mild and almost enervating with its constant sunshine and balmy atmosphere, had its influence in predisposing them to peaceful lives; and a shore rich in shell fish, and a harbor where breakers were unknown and where fish abounded, rendered it easy to obtain the necessities of life. Accordingly, with freedom from warfare, with mildness of climate, and abundance of food easily obtained, the Indians who for many generations had lived on this part of the coast had developed into a higher type than had those who lived in many other parts of California.

Coming at the time of the Spanish padres, that part of Santa Barbara County which is near the coast was thickly populated with the Indians, who were divided into small tribes, each of which lived in a separate rancheria. While some of the rancherias consisted of only a few houses, others consisted of as many as one hundred; and as there were approximately ninety rancherias within the present limits of Santa Barbara County, including those of the Islands, the native population was probably not less than fifteen thousand. Each of the tribes had a separate name which was given to the locality where it was situated. Though the names of most of the tribes are forgotten, yet a few of these names are still retained, such as: Tecolote, Lompoc, Najalayegua, Sisquoc, Suey and Tinacuac, which are the names of ranches similar to the names of the tribes that formerly occupied the land.

The rancherias were frequently built on sites which, on account of the large accumulation of shells found about them, are now known as Shell Mounds. A piece of land, slightly elevated above the beach and favorably situated for obtaining water, was generally chosen; and here were built the houses, which were conical in shape, and were constructed by planting long poles in the ground and fastening the tops together. These poles were then covered with reeds and adobe, and the earth about the house was raised to prevent the rain from entering beneath the covering. Cooking was generally done in the open air; yet in the center of the floor was the fire-place, the smoke from which escaped through an opening at the apex of the house.

Each tribe had its head; a number of tribes being united under one great chief who governed both in religious and secular affairs. In this county there was a triumvirate, of whom Yanonali ruled over the tribes dwelling between the Rincon and La Patera; Alioliquit ruled over the tribes of Dos Pueblos; and Saliapuato ruled over the tribes beyond Dos Pueblos as far as Lompoc and Santa Ynez. Yanonali was a ruler of many excellent qualities and one who exercised great control over his people. He welcomed the Spaniards and rendered them much assistance; and although sixty years of age, when he came under the influence of the padres, he was converted to Christianity, and was baptized with the name of Pedro. Salispuato, also, was very kindly disposed towards the Spaniards and rendered them very important services, particularly in hewing and bringing pine timbers from the San Rafael range. He was also noted as being the father of Tsinjuic, who was renowned for her beauty.

According to many of the accounts of the early voyagers, the Indians of the Santa Barbara Channel were far from unattractive in personal appearance, as both men and women were well formed and had regular features. Their dark brown faces were shaded by the long hair which fell to their shoulders, and within the folds of which were sometimes attached daggers of stone or flint. The men of some of the tribes wore beards of such length that they were tied in knots beneath their chins; but others were beardless and are supposed to have plucked out their beards with bivalve shells. The women had beautiful eyes, and many of them were prepossessing in appearance; yet they were modest in their bearing and agreeable in manner. They wore earrings, bracelets, and necklaces, which were made of ivory and shells; and to add to their natural attractions they painted their cheeks, and in some instances tattooed their breasts and arms. The children, who were light-hearted and playful, were of fair complexions and had light brown hair and rosy cheeks.

Owing to the equableness of the climate, the clothing was often scanty and at times exceedingly abbreviated. But although the men of some of the tribes dispensed with clothing, yet the men of other tribes wore tunics made of the skins of rabbits, deer, or seal. A few also wore jackets made of the feathered skins taken from the breasts of wild fowls. The women were more carefully clothed, and although some of them wore only short skirts of reeds, most of them were dressed in petticoats of skins, which hung from their shoulders and terminated in a heavy fringe which fell to their knees. Moccasins of deer or seal skins were worn by both sexes.

The Indians had little difficulty in obtaining food, as rabbits, deer, quail, and wild fowl were plentiful and easily trapped or shot with their arrows. Although they cultivated none of the vegetables eaten by civilized races, yet they ate acorns, which they ground into a meal and cooked, and also the wild cherry or plum, which grows very abundantly along the ridges of the Santa Ynez mountains. This fruit they called Islay, and not only the fleshy part of the cherry was eaten but also the pits, when crushed and cooked. They occasionally ate roots; and were very fond of the wild blackberry and the fruit of the tuna. The ocean furnished an abundance of fish; but the shell fish were probably the most esteemed article of diet and were consumed in large quantities. The accumulating shells were scattered about the houses and covered with layers of sand or earth; until gradually the mounds grew in height, and the half-buried houses were raised or replaced by others on the elevated surface.

Some of the principal Indian tribes lived on the Islands of Santa Cruz, Santa Rosa, and San Miguel; but after the Mission of Santa Barbara had been established, these island tribes were persuaded by the padres to move and settle near the Mission; although previously they had lived permanently on the Islands, and between them and the tribes of the Coast there was constant communication as well as barter. The boats used for crossing the channel were sufficiently large to carry one or two dozen men, and were propelled by oars. They were sharpened at both ends and made of planks, fastened carefully together by thongs of leather and wood fibre, and rendered water tight by a coating of bitumen. The Indians had canoes also, which were made from the trunk of a single tree, and were capable of carrying three or four men; and rafts made of brush and covered with thatched tules were occasionally used.

The Island of Santa Rosa has been regarded by investigators as the locality where was manufactured most of the circulating medium by which exchanges among the Indians were effected. Their money consisted of small pieces of shells, perforated and strung on a thong of leather. As the Indians were inefficient in the art of counting, the length of the string of beads and not their number was the guide to their exchange value.

The weapons of the hunt and warfare were the bow and arrow, sword, spear, and club; and were similar in construction to those used by other American tribes. Arrow heads were made of flint, porphyritic stone, and obsidian. So few, however, have been found that it is probable that they were generally made of hardened wood. The knives were of flint and obsidian, and were often carried in sheaths of skin; but the daggers and the swords were most frequently made of hardened wood, although occasionally they were made of bone or stone. Bone awls took the place of needles; and buckskin thongs of fibre, answered for thread. Smoking was habitual among the Indians, and many of the pipes used by them have been found. The bowls of the pipe were tubular in shape, and tapered gradually from the larger end of the bowl, which was about an inch or an inch and a half in diameter. They were made of serpentine or obsidian, and the mouthpiece was formed of the bone of a water fowl and securely united to the stem of the pipe with bitumen.

The utensils used for domestic purposes were primeval in construction and character, and were made almost exclusively of stone. Mortars and pestles for crushing acorns and other articles of food were in common use. The mortars were generally from nine to eighteen inches in diameter; although one, twenty-seven inches in diameter and constructed with mathematical exactness, was exhumed from an Indian grave. Vessels called Ollas, used for holding liquids and for cooking purposes, were made of steatite. They were spherical in form with small openings about one-third of the maximum diameter, and were capable of holding five or six gallons. As steatite is not found near the coast but on the Islands of Santa Rosa and Santa Catalina, these ollas were undoubtedly obtained from the island Indians in exchange for other articles. Cups and saucers made of serpentine were occasionally used, and when broken the corresponding parts were frequenly reunited by bitumen. Artifically colored baskets utilized both for cooking and for general purposes, were made of reeds, woven so closely as to make the basket waterproof; and other baskets, used for holding liquids, were bottle shaped, and were coated within and without with bitumen.

The Household furniture was extremely simple, and consisted almost exclusively of a few skins and a couch. The latter was constructed by driving into the ground four forked stakes, so as to form the corner posts of the bed, and across these were placed poles. Transversely across the poles were placed more slender ones which were covered with rushes. Skins took the place of blankets, and it is stated that comforters, made of the feathered skins of birds, were sometimes used.

The natives seem to have lacked some of the savage instincts of other races of aborigines, and open warfare between the neighboring tribes was almost unknown. They were constantly singing, dancing, and feasting; and births, marriages, or deaths were regarded as proper occasions for similar demonstrations, which were enlivened by music produced from reedlike instruments.

The men showed a higher regard for the women than was usual among most of the tribes of North American Indians. Monogamy was the prevailing custom, although the chiefs were allowed several wives. Parents arranged for the marriage of their children; and boys and girls were often betrothed in infancy, and when grown were married with formality and ceremony, of which singing, dancing, and feasting were the principal features.

In religion the Indians were polytheistic, and some of their mythology is very interesting. To Chepu, the creator, were erected wooden temples for worship; and Cabrillo relates that he saw on one of the Channel Islands wooden temples containing idols. Their religion, like that of the races of ancient history, was very closely associated with superstition, as they were constantly looking for favorable or unfavorable omens, and were influenced by their numerous sorcerers. The latter by intimidations exercised a considerable influence over the weak-minded and assumed some of the functions and privileges of the classic soothsayer.

Sickness was at times regarded as something to be alleviated by the charms practiced by the sorcerers, though generally receiving more practical consideration, as the medical value of the herbs and roots was well known; and even to-day many of the native Californians prefer these Indian remedies to the drugs of the pharmacy. The Mission padres learned the value of some of these plants and gave them Spanish names. To the trailing vine with aromatic, purplish white flowers, known in science as *Micromeria Douglasii,* they gave the name Yerba Buena, as it proved a most valuable febrifuge. The *Erydicton glutinosum,* a shrub with leaves like those of the peach and with small white or purplish flowers, was called Yerba Santa. It has proved so valuable for colds and bronchial troubles that it is now constantly used in the practice of physicians. Growing in profusion near the site of the former rancheria at Hope ranch and in many other low damp spots near Santa Barbara, is the *Anemopsis Californica,* a plant to which the padres gave the name Yerba Mansa, and which was used as a specific for many ailments. The Cascara Sagrada is known to all. Its bark was used by the Indians for rheumatism, and to-day it is gathered annually and shipped to all parts of the United States and Europe. Another plant made use of by the Indians and now well known to the medical world is the *Grindelia Robusta.* Its yellow composite flowers which appear in the late summer make it easy to be recognized. Its value is principally for pulmonary troubles, but it was formerly used in cases of skin disease also. In addition to the remedies derived from the plants, the natives utilized the *temescals,* or sweet-ovens, remains of which are occasionally found near the bank of a stream or near the ocean, to effect cures for certain illnesses.

The Indians believed in the immortality of the soul, and the dead were buried with care. Separate cemeteries were used for the men and the women; over the graves of the former were frequently erected painted poles, to which were attached human hair; and over the graves of the latter were poles, to which were attached baskets. Along the coast, in favorite spots may still be found the Indian cemeteries, which were very numerous, as every tribe had its own cemetery, which was generally very near to the village and in many instances a part of it.

On Nidever hill, near the eastern end of the city of Santa Barbara, a number of Indians were buried, and a few also were buried at Burton Mound. One of the largest Indian cemeteries was on the mesa at La Patera, and another was near Dos Pueblos. From these two latter cemeteries it has been estimated that the remains of five thousand Indians have been exhumed. At La Patera all of the indians were buried face downwards and with their heads towards the north, as if in compliance with some superstitious motive; but at Dos Pueblos they were buried without regularity. Some of the graves were surrounded by fences of wood, others by slabs of stone, or bones of whale. A peculiar feature of the burial was that their heads were often covered with ollas, many of which were so narrow at the neck that it has been a subject of wonder how the heads of the Indians were inserted into the ollas and yet remain intact. In the graves were buried weapons, utensils, and other objects, used by the Indians when alive, and which it was deemed they would require hereafter. Even the pipe and paints were not forgotten; and in one grave were found the remains of an Indian, who had been buried in his canoe, prepared to cross to the shore beyond.

Different kinds of paint were frequently found in the Indian graves. The paint was not, however, used solely for facial ornamentation, as numerous petrographs, or rock paintings, have been found among the caves and on prominent boulders, among the mountains of Santa Barbara. Perhaps the best preserved paintings are on a hollow sandstone rock that is known as La Pietra Pintada, or the Painted Rock, which is in the Santa Ynez Mountains about thirteen miles westward from the City of Santa Barbara. Here are painted representations of the sun, and of men and animals; and near the San Marcos pass, in a boulder nearly twenty feet high, is a cave upon the sides of which a checker board, suns, and anomalous forms of animal life are easily discerned. The principal pigments used in making the paintings were a red ochre, and white and black; and these were applied by rubbing the pigments against the face of the wall. The black paint has been found by analysis to be hydrous oxide of manganese; and ochres were easily obtained from the many mineral deposits found near Santa Barbara. Other painted rocks have been found near Montecito and along the coast near Gaviota. Whether these paintings were intended as hieroglyphics for the purpose of conveying definite ideas, or were simply expressions of the native artistic taste, is difficult to decide; but they have generally been found at some point frequented by the Indians.

Natives undoubtedly inhabited this coast for many generations, as their bural places would indicate. Their numbers have been generally over-estimated, yet the valleys about Santa Barbara were very populous at the time of the arrival of the first Europeans. But with the founding of the Presidio, the idle, careless life which for ages of the past they and their ancestors had lived, was with one stroke ended. Civilization, indispensable to those reared amidst its blessings, was fatal to these children of barbarism; and in a few years nearly all passed away.

The story of the lost Indian woman of San Nicholas Island well illustrates to what crude conditions of living the Indians could adapt themselves; yet how deleterious were the effects of the comforts of civilization. Formerly a large number of Indians lived on the Island, but many were exterminated by a force of Indians from Alaska, who accompanied a party of Russians on one of their periodical visits to hunt otter.

In the year 1835, a schooner, named *Peor es nada,** was sent by the padres to bring the remaining Indians to the mainland. After they were collected on the beach, prepared to embark, one of the women, noticing the absence of her child, begged the captain of the schooner to wait while she went to search for it. Before her return, a storm of great violence arose; and as there was no harbor at the island, it became necessary to set sail and run before the wind. After the storm abated, the schooner made its way to San Pedro, and the Indians were taken from there to the Mission rancherias. It was the intention of the captain of the schooner to return to the island for the woman; but he was ordered by the owners to sail for Monterey and take a cargo of lumber from that port to San Francisco. While entering the Golden Gate, the schooner was capsized and her crew were lost; and as there was no other vesssel on the southern coast sufficiently large to make the passage to San Nicholas with safety, all hope of immediately rescuing the woman was abandoned and she was soon forgotten.

In 1851, Mr. George Nidever, when visiting the island, was surprised to find, on the hard beach, human footprints the size of a woman's foot. Before he was able to make any satisfactory investigation, a strong

*Note:—The English equivalent is "Nothing is worse."

wind arose, which made his stay at the island precarious, and he returned to the mainland.

Reference to the footprints recalled to the minds of others the fact that an Indian woman had been abandoned on the island sixteen years before. In the following year Mr. Nidever returned to the island in the hope of finding her; but again a storm drove him away before meeting with any success.

In July, 1853, he again sailed for the island with a crew of men, prepared to make a thorough search. The first day spent on the island they were unsuccessful, but on the second day a basket was found; and shortly afterwards, three small huts made of ribs of the whale and covered with brush were discovered. A short distance from the huts they observed another, in which was seated an Indian woman surrounded by dogs. She presented a most strange appearance with her long hair falling over her bare shoulders, and with a garment, made of the greenish black feathered skins of the cormorant, partly covering the rest of her body. By her side were some roots, and when first noticed, she was in the act of separating some blubber from a piece of seal skin.

She had probably not seen a human being for eighteen years, and showed signs of alarm at sight of Mr. Nidever and his companions; but when they approached and showed no disposition to harm her, she arose and offered them some of the roots to eat. She had undoubtedly lost the faculty of expressing herself in language, as neither Mr. Nidever nor any of the Indians who afterward met her could understand what she said; yet when by signs he conveyed to her the idea that she was to accompany him to the mainland, she showed much pleasure and hastily gathered together her few belongings in readiness to depart. Among these were a number of water-tight vessels, similar in appearance to jars, but constructed of grass and lined with bitumen.

The party remained a month at the island, during which time she cheerfully assisted in the work; and when not otherwise engaged wove baskets of grass, which she lined with bitumen, by placing in the bottom a small portion, and upon this a pebble heated very hot. The basket was then rotated rapidly, so that the melting bitumen spread and covered the inside with a smooth coating.

Upon reaching Santa Barbara, she was taken to the home of Mr. Nidever, where she was cared for by his wife. It was supposed that her child had died, soon after she was abandoned on the island; and, evidently, her only companions were the dogs. Although never able to express herself so as to be understood, yet she was of a cheerful disposition, and frequently sang when at work. She lived, however, only a very short time after her rescue from the island, and her death was undoubtedly due to changed conditions of living.

THE EARLY EXPLORERS

AFTER the conquest of Mexico and the discovery of the Pacific several explorers, eager to emulate the success of Cortez and Balboa, sailed along the western coast of North America. One of them, Juan Roderiguez Cabrillo, was the discoverer of Alta California, and was the first European who is known to have visited the shore of Santa Barbara. He was a navigator of considerable energy and courage, and although a Portuguese by birth, was engaged in the service of Spain. Believing that the Atlantic and Pacific oceans met in such latitudes as would afford an easy communication between the old world and the new, he resolved, if possible, to make this discovery.

Accordingly, he set sail with his two ships on the 27th of June, 1542, from the Port of Navidad, Mexico. He directed his course northward, and after touching at several points of Baja California entered the harbor of San Diego, in September of that year, and thus became the discoverer of Alta California. Leaving San Diego a few days later, he continued his voyage up the coast, landing at the different islands as he passed, and touching at different points on the mainland, at each of which places he went through the formality of taking possession of the land in the name of his soverign.

About the middle of October, just fifty years after Columbus discovered America, he entered the harbor of the present City of Santa Barbara, and as he approached the shore he was met by natives, who went out in their canoes and received him with demonstrations of friendliness. It has been maintained that he landed on the beach of the present City of Santa Barbara, and was conducted by the Indians to their village, where presents were exchanged. After leaving the valley of Santa Barbara, which he described as one of great fertility, he crossed to the Islands of Santa Rosa, Santa Cruz, and San Miguel; and thence continued his way northward to a point on the coast almost within sight of the bay of San Francisco.

The severity of the winter storm made it impracticable to proceed further; and, accordingly, he returned southward and landed on the Island of San Miguel. It was his intention to winter there and recover from a recent injury to his arm; but on January 3, 1543, he died. On that little island of the Pacific, in sight of the lands of his discovery, within sound of the never-ceasing roar of the ocean, which he had made subservient to his purpose, the great explorer found a fit resting-place. No trace of his grave remains. His name and his deeds are almost forgotten.

Other voyages followed, and in the summer of 1602, Sebastian Viscaino set sail from Acapulco, with three large vessels and a transport. Under his command was a force of about two hundred men, and three Carmelite friars. He directed his course northward along the western coast of North America, and on the 12th of November, 1603, entered the harbor of San Diego, where he remained ten days. He then continued his course to the north and entered the present harbor of Santa Barbara.

One of the Carmelite friars who accompanied Viscaino, was Antonio de la Ascension, a man of considerable learning who compiled information regarding the countries visited, made maps, and gave names to the places visited. It was his custom to name each new place after the particular saint whose festival occurred on the day on which the place was entered. Consequently, the 4th of December being the anniversary of the death of Santa Barbara, her name was given to the bay which they entered that day and to the shore where the City of Santa Barbara is now located.

Some authorities claim, however, that Viscaino did not land on the shore at Santa Barbara, but that the ships were visited by the natives, who went out in their canoes and welcomed the newcomers with solemn chanting. Afterwards the chief of the Indians went aboard the ship of Viscaino with presents, and observing that the sailors were unaccompanied by their wives, and wishing to persuade them to visit his people, he offered as an inducement to give ten wives to each sailor. But as Viscaino did not regard the inducement sufficiently alluring, he continued his voyage northward and then returned to Mexico. Although he was not the first discoverer of California, yet his voyage was important on account of the maps and authentic information which he was able to furnish Europe, regarding this part of the world.

The history of the patron saint of Santa Barbara must be of interest to all who visit the city named after her; and while some discredit has been thrown upon the legend, yet it probably contains much that is true, as the essential features are in keeping with the spirit of the age when she is said to have lived. It is related that she was born in the year A. D. 218, in Nicomedia, a city of northern Asia Minor, and was a daughter of Dioscorus, a man of rank and influence among the Romans. At this time, Alexander Severus, an emperor friendly to the Christians, ruled at Rome; and it is not improbable, as is related, that Barbara was made a convert to Christianity by the famous Origen, who lived at that time. Upon the assassination of Severus and the usurpation of Maximinus, a great change took place in the treatment of the Christians by the Romans. Origen tells us that Maximinus, fearing that the Christians would avenge the death of Alexander Severus, commanded that the bishops and other Christians of influence should be killed. Acting under the authority of this edict, the pagan priests and magistrates persecuted and put to death, not only the bishops, but the Christians of all orders.

The legend of Santa Barbara relates further, that Dioscorus was one of the many who were indefatigable in their persecution. His cruelty was so extreme that Barbara, whose gentle nature had become more refined and ennobled under the influence of Christianity, besought him to spare the Christians. When, however, he discovered that she too had become one of that hated sect, he ordered her to be confined in a tower, and for a time had recourse to various arts in the hope of persuading her to abjure her religion. As he was unable in this way to accomplish his purpose, he inflicted upon her the most cruel torments, which she bore with wonderful fortitude for a girl of but seventeen years of age. At last, unable by either arts or torments to influence her, he became so enraged at his failure that he slew her with his own hand. After her death, Barbara was revered as a saint by the Christians, and among some of the nations was venerated as the patroness of artillery.

Although Viscaino had carefully examined the coast of California, and had furnished to Spain not only maps but also reports of its resources and fertility; yet so illimitable seemed the other territory that Spain had acquired in North and South America, that over a century and a half passed, before California became again an object of interest to the outside world.

Two causes finally led to a renewed interest in California. The Russians, who had acquired possessions in Alaska, began about the year 1750 to explore the Coast of California from the north, so that Spain became apprehensive that she might lose this part of her territory; and another and equally effective cause was the desire of the Franciscan order which in connection with that of the Jesuits had been most successful in building a

chain of Missions through northern Mexico and Baja
California, to establish Missions along the coast of Alta
California also.

Accordingly, in 1768, orders were issued by King
Charles III, of Spain, to the Viceroy in Mexico, that
San Diego and Monterey should be occupied and gar-
risoned; and two expeditions, one by land and one by
sea, were at once determined upon. When Father
Junipero Serra, who had charge of the Missions in Baja
California, was informed of the intended expeditions,
he at once signified his intention to accompany them in
person; and the Missions previously established were
called upon to furnish the necessary priests and church
paraphernalia, as well as the horses and cattle, required
for the new Missions.

In the following year, the expeditions set forth for
San Diego. The one by land was exposed to many
hardships; the other by sea was also not without its
misfortunes, as one of the vessels lost its bearings, and
sailing too far northward landed by mistake on one of
the islands which form Santa Barbara Channel. On
the beach of this island the padres lost a small iron
cross, which was found by the natives, who returned it,
as the vessel was about to sail, and in commemoration
of this circumstance, the island was called Santa Cruz.

After the founding of San Diego Mission, Governor
Portola, Father Serra, and Sergeant Ortega, who subsequently became *comandante* of the Santa Barbara
pueblo, marched northward along the coast to Monterey, passing, en route, the present site of Santa Barbara,
which they named San Joaquin de la Laguna.

Monterey, being founded, other Missions were speed-
ily established along the coast in the southern and cen-
tral parts of the state; but the country bordering on
Santa Barbara channel was the last to receive the attention of Spain. In 1775, however, Felipe de Neve,
who had hitherto been only nominal governor, received

his commission from the king of Spain as governor of California, with instructions to make Monterey the seat of his government. As none of the Missions lying between San Diego and Monterey were protected by presidios, Neve realized the importance of establishing a presidio and Mission on the Santa Barbara Channel; and with the sanction of the king of Spain and the assistance of Junipero Serra, preparations were made to accomplish this object. Although delayed in carrying out his plans, in the spring of 1782, the Mission of San Buenaventura was founded; and it was then decided to at once found another Mission on the Channel ten leagues further to the north, and to build a presidio at such place as should be determined upon, for the protection of the channel Missions.

THE PRESIDIO

About the middle of April, 1782, Captain Jose Francisco Ortega, in command of fifty men and accompanied by Governor Neve and Father Junipero Serra, left the newly founded Mission of San Buenaventura and marched along the coast between the ocean and the high cliffs which flank the ocean side. There were no roads in those days, but Indian trails extended along the beach. Indian villages were met with here and there; and when the pioneers crossed the Rincon Creek and entered the fertile valley of Carpinteria, these villages became more numerous. At last they reached the lagoon which formerly existed in the lower part of this city and covered the present estero, reaching up to the old De la Guerra gardens. Passing around the lagoon, they found on its western side a large Indian village, to which the name San Joaquin de la Laguna had previously been given, and which was ruled over by Yanonali. Here it was decided the new presidio should be built.

The 21st day of April, 1782, was the natal day of Santa Barbara. It is not difficult to relate what occurred on that memorable morning, for what the records fail to mention is supplied by a knowledge of what occurred at the founding of other presidios. The soldiers, with faces bronzed by exposure and clad in leathern waistcoats and leggins, were assembled near the intersection of Canon Perdido and Santa Barbara streets, where now only a few of the old buildings, crumbling to dust and forgotten, remain to mark the site of the presidio. From the many rancherias throughout the valleys the Indians had come, impelled by curiosity and awe; and it must have been with intense interest that they watched the newcomers and wondered at their purpose.

Father Junipero, clad in alb and stole, stood in a hastily constructed chapel of brush before a roughly hewn table used as an altar. The soldiers, under the command of, Governor Neve and Captain Ortega then formed in a square, and having laid aside their shields and lances, knelt with bared heads while the reverend Father with uplifted hands invoked the blessings of heaven upon the congregation and their undertaking. After the dedication of the spot, the cross was raised, mass was celebrated, and an impressive sermon was preached. With these simple ceremonies was founded the City of Santa Barbara; and a record of the events, in the handwriting of Junipero Serra and signed by himself, is preserved among the old archives of the parochial church.

It was the expectation of Junipero Serra, who was entirely absorbed in the advancement of the Church, that as soon as temporary dwellings were provided for the accommodation of the soldiers, work would be commenced on the founding of the Mission; but Neve felt that their position among unknown tribes would be insecure until the fortifications and buildings of the presidio had been at least partly completed; and, therefore, declined to take any immediate steps towards the founding of the Mission. The venerable Serra was greatly disappointed at the decision, and shortly afterwards left Santa Barbara for the Mission of San Carlos, which he had founded at Monterey. He was nearly seventy years of age, yet he traveled all the distance on foot, as was his custom. It was his last long journey, and there on the 28th of August, 1784, he died.

The name of Junipero Serra deserves more than a passing notice, as it is inseparably connected with the founding of the Missions of California, the influence of which, in enlightening the crude minds of the natives, has perhaps been too little appreciated. Serra was born on November 24th, 1713, at Petra, in the island of Majorca, and was baptized as Miguel Jose, but he assumed the name of Junipero when he became a monk of the order of Franciscans. At the time that the Jesuits were expelled from Mexico, and the Missions which they had built in Baja California were turned over to the Franciscans, Serra, who was then living in Mexico, was made the *presidente* of those Missions. When he began the task of founding the Missions of Alta California, he was about fifty-five years of age, tall, and erect in stature; and although his constitution had been enfeebled by constant vigils and fasting, yet he possessed both the indomitable perserverance and energy essential to the accomplishment of such an undertaking. In his efforts, he was actuated by none but the purest and most disinterested of motives, regarding himself as a chosen instrument for the conversion of the Indians. His self-imposed penances and acts of contrition were worthy of a monk of the Middle Ages; and the high esteem and affection with which he was regarded is best attested by the manner in which the news of his death was received. When he ceased to breathe, and the tolling bells of San Carlos Mission conveyed the sad news, the whole population mourned. A weeping crowd of soldiers and neophites assembled at his bier, and forming a long procession, carried he remains and placed them before the altar, where they remained in state until borne to their final resting place.

After the religious ceremonies of dedicating the presidio had been performed, temporary lodgings of brush and mud were prepared for the soldiers; and these were surrounded by a palisade, constructed of branches of oak and sycamore trees, making an enclosure of about sixty square yards. The foundation of the permanent presidio was then begun on a slight eminence, about fifty feet above the level of the sea, and flanked on the

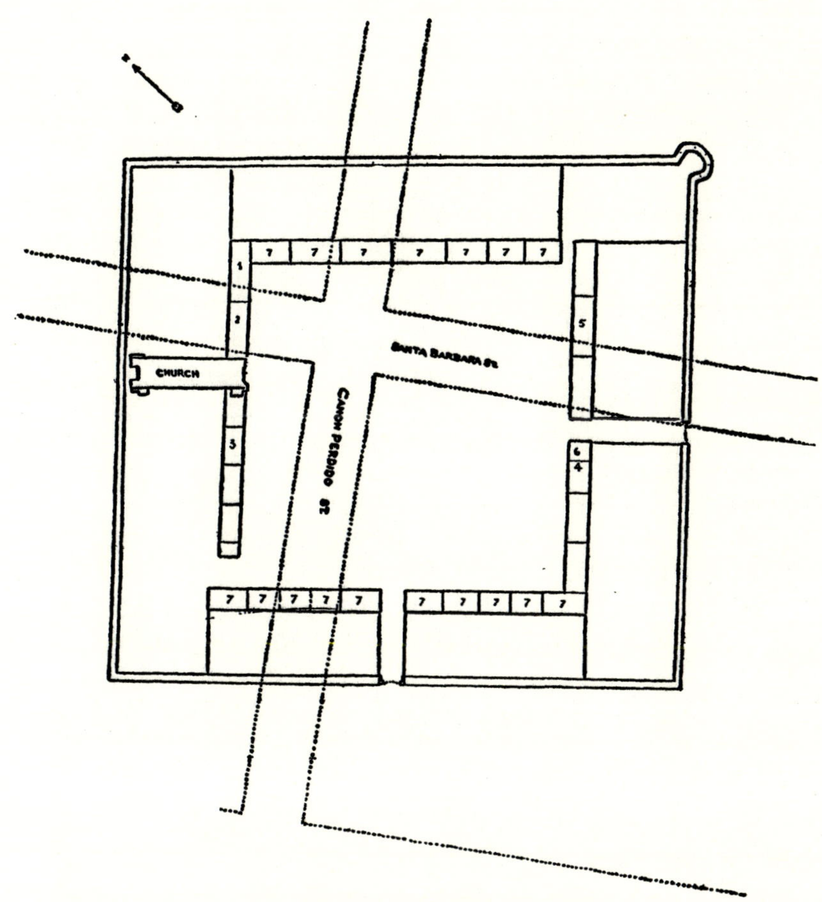

PLAT OF THE PRESIDIO

1 Comandante   3 Sergeant's House   6 Guard House
2 Alferez   4 Quartermaster   7 Soldiers'
     5 Store House   Quarters

left by the lagoon, which approached near to one of the walls. The exact location is easily determined by reference to the Sloyd school which occupies what was the easterly corner.

The plan of the presidio was simple; yet, when carried out, showed how admirably it was adapted to the purposes for which it was designed. The buildings were constructed about the sides of an open piece of ground approximately three hundred and twenty feet square, the front of the buildings forming unbroken lines facing the square, and the rear of the buildings forming a wall. For additional protection, an outer wall was planned to surround the buildings and leave an open space about eighty feet in depth between it and the buildings. Thus, if the enemy had been able to surmount the outer wall, they would still have been confronted with the almost solid wall formed by the rear of the houses, and exposed to the fire of the soldiers from the openings, used as windows.

It must not be assumed that the presidio was laid out with the scientific exactness, or that the proportions of the several buildings conformed to any arbitrary standard, as the drawings of some historians would incline us to believe. The little force which founded and built the presidio was unaccompanied by either engineer or architect, so that the walls lacked the mathematical exactness of right-angled parallelograms; and the buildings were of slightly different lengths and heights. But the difficuties under which the builders worked should atone for any such irregularities which added to the interesting appearance of the presidio, rather than detracted from it.

The permanent buildings were substantially built of adobe and mortar, resting on solid stone foundations. The first to be erected occupied the northeast and southwest sides of the quadrangle, and were used as dwelling houses for the soldiers. The main entrance, which was on the side towards the ocean, was about twenty feet in width and was always carefully guarded. To the right of this entrance, were the storehouses; and on the left the guardhouse and also the house of the sergeant. Directly facing the entrance, and on the northwest side of the square, was the church, the high roof of which, surmounted by a wooden cross, made it the most noticeable structure of the presidio. The rest of this side was occupied by the dwellings of the officers, of which that of the *comandante* occupied the position farthest to the right and at the northerly corner of the square.

The outer wall which surrounded the buildings was built of adobe, resting on a foundation of stone, and had a thickness of seven feet and a height of twelve feet. In addition to the main entrance, there was a small opening in the southwest side of the wall, which was frequently used, but which could be easily closed, in case of necessity. At the easterly corner of the presidio was erected a bastian, in which was stationed a small iron cannon. Two other iron pieces and one brass six-pounder, which were placed in the square facing the entrance, completed the artillery.

As the Mexicans were most expert riders, and as a very large country was under the protection of but a handful of soldiers, it was but natural that they should be prepared to be converted at any moment into a company of cavalry. Accordingly, the spaces on both sides of the main entrance and between the buildings and outer wall were used as corrals, where the horses could be stabled.

The garrison was supplied by springs of water, near at hand; but as a precaution against a siege, a well was sunk in one corner of the square. With a supply of water and with storehouses filled with grain, with cannon for protection against attack, and horses ready for sallies, this small force of light-armed soldiers was well prepared to protect itself against many thousands of unwarlike Indians, armed only with bows and arrows; yet the presidio of Santa Barbara was but an outpost in the wilderness; and was over two hundred miles distant from the nearest neighboring presidios, where equally small garrisons were located. Unknown dangers surrounded this handful of men, yet they were filled with the enthusiasm of Argonauts; and to add to their cheer, from the center of he square rose a flagpole, from which floated, at first, the colors of Spain, and, later, those of the Mexican Republic.

Although the plan of the presidio was simple, and the soldiers were assisted by a few sailors, yet the work at first, progressed slowly; later, however, it advanced more rapidly when by offering food and clothing Captain Ortega secured the services of the Indians, who were most useful, not only for procuring fish and game, but also for making adobe bricks, and hewing and hauling timbers. Gradually the mud and brick huts were replaced by solid adobe structures, faced with mortar and brightened with a coat of whitewash; the cane and thatched roofs were covered with red tiles; and heavy oaken doors, which could be secured in case of attack, were hung in the exits at the rear of the buildings. Yet every part of the strucures was necessarily simple. The windows were merely small openings in the sides of the walls, which could be closed by wooden shutters; the hardened ground, on which may have been thrown the skin of a deer, was the only flooring; and all of the furnishings were exceedingly meagre. Each of the separate houses consisted of two or more dwelling rooms, to which in several instances a kitchen was subsequently attached, although the cooking was often conducted in the open air.

In 1793, just eleven years after the foundation had been begun, the governor referred to the Santa Barbara presidio as being in the best condition of any in Cali-

One of the Original Houses of the Soldiers in the Presidio

fornia. All of the houses were roofed; the outer wall was erected; and the presidio was completed with the exception of the church, which was begun shortly after. In 1797 it was finished, and was dedicated on the festive day of Saint Guadalupe. It was the first church erected in Santa Barbara, and for more than half a century, divine services were held within its walls. It was an adobe building twenty-four feet in width with a depth of sixty feet, exclusive of the sacristy. The interior was adorned with statuary and paintings; and many years later, but previous to the year 1826, it was furnished with an organ. Until the present parish church was erected in 1854, it was attended not only by the soldiers but by the residents of the pueblo. It was the first object to atract attention, as one entered the presidio, and was still standing, long after the fortifications had crumbled away. Adjoining the church, but without the presidio walls, was the burial ground, where the soldiers and the first settlers were buried until the year 1818, when a cemetery was established near the foothills.

Some of the adobe buildings which formed the southwest side of the quadrangle and which were occupied by the soldiers and their families are still standing, and with the exception of the temporary huts, they were the first buildings to be erected in Santa Barbara, although much over a century old. Another of the original buildings, that was used for officers' quarters and was located on the northwest side of the square, is now so modified that it has lost much of that appearance of age which is characteristic of the other buildings, but may still be found at the rear of a more modern house facing on Canon Perdido street. These and the house of the commandante which is located three or four rods north-westerly from the corner of Santa Barbara and Canon Perdido streets are the only remaining buildings of the presidio.

No effort has been made to modernize the houses on the southwest side of the square. They bear the unmistakable evidences of age; yet the sun and rain of over a hundred years have failed to wear away the adobe walls. Beneath the tiles appear the cane and thatched roofs that were placed there over a century ago, and many of the doors and windows remain as they were when the presidio was built. Of the rest of the presidio nothing remains but the occasional tracings of the outer walls. Every indication of the cemetery has been effaced. The bells and relics of the old presidio church have been removed to the present parochial church, while the ruined walls and houses have given back to earth the soil, from which they were made. Yet in the days of its prosperity, the presidio of Santa Barbara, with its regular and well-constructed houses, white walls, and red tiled roofs, presented a more favorable appearance than that of any other settlement along the coast.

Until the discovery of gold in California and the consequent growth of San Francisco and the cities of the interior of the state, Santa Barbara was one of the most important places in Alta California. The whole of the territory occupied by the missionaries was divided into four districts, in each of which was built a presidio; and the officers of these presidios had both military and civil jurisdiction over their respective districts. The presidio of Santa Barbara had jurisdiction over the Missions of La Purissima, Santa Ynez, Santa Barbara, San Buenaventura, San Fernando, and the pueblo of La Reyna de los Angeles. Though the most important of the presidios was at Monterey, as it was the official seat of the governor and the territorial deputation; the presidio of Santa Barbara was undoubtedly next in importance, and its officers had considerable prestige in the government of the territory. There seemed to be an established rule that, in the event of the death of the governor, the comandante of Santa Barbara should succeed as acting governor, until an appointment should be made. This happened when upon the death of Governor Jose Arrellago, Jose Arguello, the comandante of Santa Barbara, became governor; and Pablo Vicenti de Sola, when taken ill during his administration as governor, provided that in case of his death, Jose De la Guerra, who was at that time comandante at Santa Barbara, should succeed him as governor. The district of Santa Barbara seems to have been the richest in cattle, hides, and tallow, which constituted almost the only commodities of trade that California then had. About the year 1825, the territory under the jurisdiction of Santa Barbara had probably not less than 300,-000 head of cattle and 25,000 head of horses, although these numbers rapidly decreased after the secularization. The appropriation that was made from the royal treasury for the presidio of Santa Barbara, previous to the independence of Mexico, amounted approximately to $15,000 per annum, and was expended, principally, in the maintenance of about sixty soldiers. These however, were divided among the different Missions of the district, so that a force not much exceeding half that number remained at the presidio.

The officers of the presidio were civil as well as military and consisted of the *comandante,* or commander, who had sometimes the rank of lieutenant but generally that of captain; of an *alcade,* or justice of the peace; of an *alfarez,* or ensign; and the *habilitado,* who had charge of all branches of the revenue and was generally postmaster. The duties of habilitado were frequently discharged by the comandante.

The first comandante was Captain Jose Francisco Ortega, who for two years was engaged in the work of building the presidio and laying the foundation upon which rested the future prosperity of this district. While he may have been severe in the exercise of his office, yet he was a man of indomitable energy and untiring in his efforts to establish a presidio in which no essential should be wanting. One of his enterprises was the construction of a stone reservoir, and a ditch through which the water from Mission Creek was conducted for irrigation purposes; and through his efforts farming was begun on a large scale upon the land adjoining the presidio. An orchard was planted beyond its western wall, and three or four fruit trees that were subsequently planted in this orchard are still alive. His attention was also directed to stock raising, and through his efforts the presidio acquired a number of horses and cattle, the first of which came from San Buenaventura; and within a few years they multiplied very rapidly. After being in command for two years, Ortega was removed to assume other important duties, and at one time was comandante of Monterey. His life had always been an active one. He was born in the state of Guanajuato, Mexico, and engaged in mining in early life, but subsequently drifted to Baja California, where he entered the military service. He accompanied the expedition under Governor Portola in 1769, the object of which was to found the Missions of Alta California; and rendered signal service to these first pioneers, in exploring the way among the Indian tribes of the coast. After serving as comandante at Santa Barbara and Monterey, he continued to perform military duty until shortly before his death. He was beloved by the people of Santa Barbara, and when he died was sincerely mourned.

In 1784 Ortega was succeeded in command by Captain Felipe de Goycoechea, who was the comandante at Santa Barbara until 1802. During his term of office the presidio and most of the Mission buildings were finished. After leaving Santa Barbara, Goycoechea was made governor of Baja California.

Goycoechea was succeeded by Lieutenant Raimundo Carrillo, who for five years was comandante at the presidio, and discharged the duties of his office with firmness yet clemency. This period was rendered memorable by the earthquakes of 1806, which damaged not only some of the buildings of the Mission, but also the presidio chapel. The walls of the latter were badly cracked; and a severe gale, two months later, almost completely destroyed the edifice.

Carrillo was born in 1749, at Lorto, the capital of Baja California; and came to Alta California about twenty years later, at which time he became a soldier. He served as a corporal, at Monterey, and later as a sergeant, at Santa Barbara. Shortly afterwards he was made lieutenant and comandante at Monterey; and two years later was comandante at Santa Barbara. He was a very efficient officer and a man of much intelligence.

Carrillo was succeeded in command by Captain Jose Dario Arguello, who for nine years was comandante at Santa Barbara. One of the most important acts of his administration was the opening of common schools; but unfortunately they received but little public support, although several excellent instructors were secured. As he was enterprising and public-spirited, he would have accomplished much more during his administration were it not for the disastrous earthquakes which began in December, 1812, and recurred with frequency until March of the following year. These earthquakes were the severest recorded in the history of Southern California; and considerable damage was done to every Mission along the coast from Purissima, at Lompoc, to San Juan Capistrano near San Diego. At Purissima, not only the church and some of the Mission buildings but a great many of the Indian houses were completely demolished. At San Juan Capistrano, the new stone church which was finished the preceding year was destroyed; and nearly all of the fifty people who were attending mass on the morning when the first severe earthquake occurred were killed.

At Santa Barbara, a number of the Mission buildings were totally destroyed; and the damage to the presidio buildings was so extensive, that the re-building of the presidio on a different site was seriously contemplated. It is stated that the earth opened in many places, and that a tidal wave broke upon the shore. Though many of the reports were doubtless exaggerated, yet for several weeks the greatest consternation prevailed among the people; and even the ensign wrote the governor that he was convulsed with fear.

Captain Arguello was born in Queretaro, Mexico, in 1755, and at twenty years of age enlisted as a soldier. He rose to be a captain through his intrinsic worth, and became one of the most influential men in California, where he resided for thirty-four years. For a short time he was acting governor of Alta California, and, subsequently, served for several years as governor of Baja California.

Arguello was succeeded, in 1815, by Captain Jose Antonio De la Guerra y Noriega, whose military command extended over a period of twenty-four years, during which the presidio passed through the best days of its existence. At the time he assumed command, the presidio was completed and was in the best condition of any in California; all of the Mission buildings had been erected, with the exception of the present stone church, which was founded the same year and completed five years later; the pueblo had begun to spring up around the presidio; and some of the Mexican soldiers had received grants of ranches. Santa Barbara had reached a position of dignity and importance among the settlements of the Pacific Coast. Although Monterey was the capital of Alta California, the governors frequently visited Santa Barbara, and several gubernatorial proclamations were made during their visits here. Meetings of territorial officials were also occasionally held at the presidio, and its comandante was a man of consequence in the affairs of the coast.

Entirely isolated from the civilized world, startling events at Santa Barbara were few; yet so widely scattered were the settlements and the population of each was so small, that events which now might seem of most trivial importance appeared then fraught with the gravest consequences. One of the interesting events which occurred during the command of Captain de La Guerra, and for several days occasioned much excitement in this peaceful spot, was the visit to the California coast of two piratical vessels.

The first news of the threatened invasion was received from a sea captain by the name of Henry Gyzelaar, who two years before had been arrested by Captain De la Guerra, on the charge of smuggling; but was shortly afterwards released upon proving his innocence. Pending the investigation, he remained at the home of De la Gurra in the presidio, where he received such courteous treatment that he left Santa Barbara with feelings of gratitude towards his captor. In the fall of 1818, he arrived unexpectedly at Santa Barbara in his sailing vessel and announced to De la Guerra, that he had come direct from the Hawaiian Islands, where Hippolyte Bouchard, a Frenchman, was fitting out two vessels with an armament of fifty-four guns and manned by two hundred and fifty men, with the design of preying on this coast.

The swiftest courier was at once dispatched to the governor; and the several presidios and Missions of the Coast were warned of the danger. Father Ripoll, the superior of the Santa Barbara Mission, organized an Indian force of one hundred and eighty men to co-operate with the soldiers of the presidio; but as the Indians were untrained and as the few small guns of the presidio, and of the *castillo* on the Mesa, would be of little avail in opposing the armament of the two vessels, orders were issued that the women and children should be prepared for flight to Santa Ynez; that all articles of value should be packed ready for shipment; and that the cattle should be driven inland, as soon as the vessels were sighted.

Bouchard first appeared near Monterey, where some firing occurred between the vessels and a small battery on the shore; and the governor reported that several of the attacking party were killed in the engagement. On the following day, the pirates landed and carried away some cattle, and then sailed southward and landed at the rancho Del Refugio, about thirty miles from Santa Barbara. This ranch, at that time, was the most interesting and productive of any ranch in Santa Barbara County, and a force of thirty mounted soldiers was hastily sent from the pueblo to render assistance; but before they could arrive, the ranch was plundered; the buildings were burned; and the cattle which had not been driven into the mountains were killed. Although unable to offer any resistance, some of the Mexicans, who were hiding in ambush, captured three of the pirates.

When news was received at Santa Barbara of the plundering of the rancho Del Refugio and of the approach of the vessels, the greatest excitement prevailed. The women were hastily sent over the mountain trails to Santa Ynez; valuables were concealed; and Captain De la Guerra prepared to make all possible resistance. Bouchard arrived at Santa Barbara on the 6th of December; but, to the surprise of everyone, did not attempt to land. He evidently realized that nothing could be gained by an attack, as there had been sufficient opportunity to remove all valuables and drive away the cattle; and, accordingly, a message was sent on shore with a flag of truce and an exchange of prisoners proposed. This offer was finally accepted; and, the exchange being effected, the pirates sailed away.

In 1821, during the command of De la Guerra, Mexico declared its independence and Alta California became a territory of the republic. A few years after the independence of Mexico was declared, an amusing incident occurred at Santa Barbara, which well illustrates how isolated California then was from the rest of the world, as a result of the difficulties of communication and travel. Three cadets, belonging to the most prominent families of Santa Barbara, but with identities disguised and dressed as Spanish officers, rang the bell of the presidio one morning, and after receiving the salute of the guard, announced that they had just arrived in a Spanish ship, lying at anchor in the harbor; and that in the name of their king, who, they claimed, had regained sovereignty over Mexico and its territories, they would take possession of the presidio. In great consternation a few loyal Mexicans of the garrison whose latest information received from the Mexican capital was three or four months old, and who, consequently, were not in a position to know the truth, sounded the alarm, loaded the cannon, and prepared for a siege. The situation then began to look so serious that the cadets confessed their identity and acknowledged that the Spanish invasion was a joke.

Captain De la Guerra was by birth and in feelings a Spaniard, whereas, most of the officers in California were Mexicans; and this difference in birth occasioned some little jealousy, had it not been for this, he would probably have been governor, as he was both able and popular. He was born in Spain, in 1779, of a distinguished family, and when still very young went to Mexico, where an uncle lived. Shortly afterwards, he entered the army as a cadet and occupied several military positions, until, in 1806, he was promoted to be lieutenant of the Santa Barbara Company. In 1810 he was chosen habilitado general of both Californias and sent to Mexico; but he was arrested by Mexican insurgents, and being unable to reach the City of Mexico, he returned to Santa Barbara. In 1815, he was appointed comandante of the Santa Barbara Company, which office he occupied much of the time until 1842. Soon after being made comandante, he was promoted to be captain, the duties of which office he discharged with such satisfaction that he was subsequently offered many other important offices. His wife, Maria Antonia Carrillo, was a daughter of Comandante Carrillo, and their fourth son, Pablo De la Guerra, was state senator and lieutenant governor. During his long life Captain De la Guerra exercised a strong influence in the political affairs of Alta California. He died in 1858, and was buried at the Mission.

During part of the years 1828 and 1829, when De la Guerra was absent in Mexico, Lieutenant Raimundo Pacheco acted as comandante of Santa Barbara. He was born in Guanajuato, Mexico, and was acting commander at Monterey before being transferred to Santa Barbara. He was an efficient and brave officer of high character, but was killed while still young. He left a son, Romualdo, who became very prominent in California, after its admission to the Union, and occupied many offices, including those of lieutenant governor and acting governor of this state.

De la Guerra was succeeded as comandante by Gumesindo Flores, a Mexican and brevet lieutenant-colonel, who was comandante at Monterey from 1839 to 1842, when he was transferred to Santa Barbara. Flores was actively engaged in territorial affairs during his short term as comandante at Santa Barbara, and is frequently regarded as the last comandante, although Raimundo Carrillo was acting commander, during his absence for part of the year 1846. In December of that year, Fremont crossed the Santa Ynez mountains and entered

Santa Barbara with his battalion of Americans. The presidio had played a most important and useful part in the early settlement of this section of the coast, but with the coming of Fremont its days of glory were over.

THE MISSION

FIRST DECADE

ALTHOUGH the construction of the presidio continued uninterruptedly from the beginning, four years had passed, before it was so far advanced that the comandante felt that part of his men could be spared for work on the Mission. Previous experience had shown the wisdom of locating the Mission at a moderate distance from the presidio, but it would have been impossible to have chosen a better or more beautiful site than the present one on the south bank of Pedregosa creek at the base of the foothills. On the 4th of December, 1786 which was the anniversary of the feast of Santa Barbara, and the founding of the presidio; just ten years and five months after the American colonists on the Atlantic Coast had proclaimed their political independence; the ground was consecrated and the cross was raised. A few days later Francisco de Lasuen, the *presidente* of the Californian Missions, attended by Governor Fages and a few of the officers and soldiers from the presidio, held divine services beneath a bower of green branches, which had been erected on the site. The founding of the Mission was then practically begun; but on account of winter storms the actual construction of the building was delayed until the following spring.

It was desirable that, as far as possible, the Mission settlement should not rely upon the presidio, excepting for protection in case of attack; and that this condition of independence should be effected without unnecessary delay. Therefore, a large number of the men who had been engaged in constructing the building of the presidio gave their entire attention to the work at the Mission; and many buildings were completed during the first year after it was founded.

The first building to be erected occupied the position of the present structure, to the left of the Mission Church, and was for the use of the priests. It was built of adobe with walls two and a half feet in thickness, resting on stone foundations. The length was forty-five feet and the depth was fifteen feet; and adjoining it was a kitchen, eighteen feet by fifteen feet in dimensions. After completing this building, the first Mission church was built. It had a breadth of fifteen feet and depth of forty-five feet, and like the dwelling was built with adobe walls and stone foundations. Its peaked roof was made of rafters, across which slender poles tied to the rafters by thongs of leather were thickly laid. The poles were then covered with a layer of mud, and over this was placed a superstructure of thatch. The following year, the thatch was replaced by red tiles, and the church was slightly enlarged.

As soon as the church was finished, a small house was built for the Indian servants and a large one for the unmarried women. A granary and a carpenter shop were then built; but it was found necessary to temporarily use the former as a general storehouse, and the latter as a bunkhouse for some of the workmen. A building seventy-five feet in length by seventeen feet in depth, and consisting of four rooms, was also erected that year and used as a permanent dwelling house for the lay brothers; a church; dwellings for the priests, lay brothers, unmarried women, and servants; a kitchen; a granary; and a carpenter shop, were the principal results of the work during the first year.

The plan adopted at the presidio of constructing buildings of adobe about an open square, was followed at the Mission; and during the second and third years, the sides of the quadrangle facing the ocean and the southwest were finished. Shortly aferwards, the remaining two sides were finished, the northeast side occupying the present site of the Mission church. The additional buildings consisted principally of larger apartments for the priests, and better accommodations for the unmarried women and girls. It was also found necessary to add more storehouses; in some of which were kept the grain and general provisions; and in others were kept the fuel, the agricultural implements, and the *alforjas* and harness of the pack animals. After these buildings were finished, there was added a large weaving room where the Indian women were instructed in the art of weaving.

As it was intended that the buildings should be permanent, the foundations of all of them were made of stone cemented with mortar; and the walls of the buildings were of adobe plastered with mortar, which rendered them less suseptible to the influence of the weather. The lime used was from calcareous deposits, found near by; and was burnt in kilns, some of which may still be found in the canyon beyond the mission. Many changes in the buildings, however, were made from time to time to render them more permanent and convenient. In the second year, the manufacture of tiles began, and the thatched roofs were recovered with them. The rafters, originally used, were of sycamore and poplar, which grew in abundance near at hand; but a few years later they rotted, and were replaced by rafters of pine. These were obtained with great difficulty and labor, as most of them were brought by the Indians from the mountains beyond the Santa Ynez river.

In 1795, the part of the square facing the presidio was improved by the addition of a corridor, running the whole length of the front, the tile roof of which was supported by pillars of brick and mortar. Some attention was then given to the appearance of the inner court which is now called the Mission Garden.   It was one hundred and forty feet square, and within its seclusion the padres spent a great part of their time, during the hours of recreation and light labor.   Three years later, in 1800, they built a corridor which extended around three of its sides.   The flooring was paved with red square tiles; and the roof, which was supported on columns of brick and mortar, was also covered with tiles.

The Mission buildings now began to assume an appearance of importance; yet all of them were but one story high, and an adobe church occupied the site of the present stone church.   The work of construction which had begun under most favorable auspices continued from year to year with but little interruption; and after the completion of the dwelling houses, many larger storehouses also were built for the grain and corn which were harvested in the fertile valleys to the west of the Mission.

In 1789, there were over three hundred Indians at the Mission, all of whom were required to regularly attend church services.   Although the number of other buildings was increased with the growing population; yet it was undesirable to have more than one church; and when the first church, after being enlarged, was found to be too small, it was torn down and a new one erected.   It was located a short distance from the south corner of the Mission quadrangle; and a part of the stone foundation, which has been removed to the level of the ground, may still be seen about fifty feet to the south of the large stone fountain, near the terminus of the present car line.   In construction this church was similar to the first, but was much larger, having a length of ninety feet and a breadth of fifteen feet.

But even the new church was soon found to be inadequate to the increasing numbers of converts, and in 1793 the third church was begun on the site of the present Mission church and completed in the following year.

Although of adobe, it was far more pretentious than the former one.   It was about twenty-seven feet in width and one hundred and thirty feet in depth, not including the sacristy, which was twenty-seven feet by fifteen feet. In front of the church was a pavement made of flat tiles similar to those in front of the present church; the walls were plastered with mortar, and the roof was covered with tiles.   Within, were six chapels, in each were hung large oil paintings, which had been brought from Spain.

Could we look back and see the Mission buildings as they were at the end of the first decade, we should see an interesting picture, the result of ten years of hard toil; although a picture quite different in completeness from what it was twenty years later. We should see, surrounding a square, rows of low buildings all one story in height and with a depth of nearly twenty feet. Their sides were whitened and the roofs were covered with red tiles.   On the ocean side was a corridor covered with a roof of tiles; and the light that streamed in at the outer windows of the rooms, which were but one tier in depth, passed through the windows on the other side to the corridor that surrounded the inner court. At one corner of this square was located the church.

The square was the nucleus of the Mission settlement, and at the end of the first decade comprised nearly all the buildings.   Beyond its protecting walls were only a few storehouses and outhouses where work was done. But scattered here and there on the higher bank and even beyond the creek below, were the rude huts of the Indians who had not yet been entirely subdued.

The work that had been accomplished during the first decade ending in December, 1796, might be summarized as follows:

December 4, 1786 Founding of the Mission of Santa Barbara.

1787: The first church and first buildings about the

square were built. The number of the Indians at the
Mission was one hundred and eighty-three.

1788: Tiles were manufactured; granaries were
built; and the church was enlarged. The number of
Indians was three hundred and seven.

1789: The second church and more granaries were
built. The number of Indians was four hundred and
twenty-five.

1790: Two dwelling houses for the priests were built,
and one of the sides of the square, which consisted of a
large house one hundred and seventy-five feet in length
by eighteen feet in depth, and contained a kitchen, din-
ing room, assembly hall, and storeroom, was completed.
A large granary was also built. The number of Indians
was four hundred and seven.

1791: A guard house, carpenter shop, and other out
houses were built.

1792: Large corrals were built. The number of Indians was five hundred.

1793: The third church was commenced.

1794: The third church was finished, and a granary
and weavery were built.

1795: The work of replacing the rafters of the houses
about the square was begun.

1796: The work on the rafters was finished, and a
corridor was built on the side of the square facing the
presidio. The number of Indians at the Mission was
now six hundred and forty-six.

SECOND DECADE

During the second decade in the Mission history, beginning with the year 1797, the buildings began to ac-
quire such proportions and completeness as characterized their best days. The most important events that
occurred during this period were the construction of
rows of buildings about the second or inner square; the
construction of large granaries; the building of the Ind-

ian village; the planting of orchards; the building of tanneries; and the construction of the first reservoir.

The growing needs of the settlement required the erection of more buildings; and in 1797, the second square was marked out, adjacent to the first square and on its northwest side. The new square, when finished, was about the same size as the first square with which it was connected and was similar to it in appearance. While the new square was used for the Indians employed in domestic work at the Mission, the old square was thereafter reserved for the exclusive use of the padres. Three granaries, each seventy-five feet in length; a leather shop; a blacksmith shop; a house for poultry; and general storehouses, were built about the sides of the new square.

Although some of the grain was stored in the buildings about the inner square, yet it became necessary to build other storehouses; and two years later another granary, twenty feet in breadth and one hundred and thirty feet in length, was built. Such large storehouses became necessary as large amounts of grain were now raised. During the first year of its existence, the Mission of Santa Barbara was dependent upon the neighboring Missions for provisions, but as soon as the most necessary buildings had been erected the padres began cultivating the land. At first most of the grain was raised in the fertile valleys between the Arroyo Pedregosa and the Arroyo del Burro, but later the Mission had many ranches extending from the Rincon to Gaviota. The low bottom lands were used for raising the corn and grain, while the rolling hills were generally reserved for the flocks and herds. From San Buenaventura the padres brought horses, mules, cattle, and sheep; all of which increased rapidly, and in a few years were numbered by the tens of thousands.

The inherited traits and disposition of the Indian render him unsuitable for occupations associated with

The Mission of Santa Barbara as it Probably Appeared in 1798

close confinement; but in watching and herding cattle and in farming lands, the natives proved serviceable to the padres. Still in order to inculcate the ways of civilization, the padres gradually allotted them services of a more trying nature. The men were employed in making tiles and working in the tanneries; and the women were taught to weave the wool and to make blankets and cloth. The latter, which was of a better quality than most of the cloth produced in Mexico, was then made into garments for which there was a great demand; as it was required at the Mission that all of the Indians should be decently clad, while upon the first arrival of the padres, they lived almost entirely without any clothing.

There were now about eight hundred Indians living in scattered huts in the vicinity of the Mission. As they were beginning to feel the enervating influences of civilization, it was desirable that they should have comfortable homes and the safety of the padres required that homes should be so located that the actions of the Indians could be observed and restrained in case of an outbreak. It was also necessary in order to successfully Christianize them and inculcate the principles of civilization that they should be under the constant restraint of the padres. Accordingly, in the year 1798, a piece of land about three hundred and fifty feet in breadth by seven hundred feet in length, on the southwest side of the Mission, and extending across the present Garden street was set apart for the exclusive use of the Indians, and during the next eight years, approximately two hundred and fifty houses were erected within this space.

The principal houses were built in three rows of three tiers in depth; and as the rows and tiers were separated by the longitudinal and cross streets, there were accordingly nine separate blocks of houses. The longitudinal streets had a breadth of sixty feet and the cross streets a breadth of thirty-five feet. The houses

1 Thrashing Floor
2 Weavery
3 Granary
4 Inner Court
5 Settling Tank
6 Upper Reservoir
7 Mill
8 Lower Reservoir
9 House for Manufacturing Pottery
10 Cow Shed
11 Vats for Tanning
12 Home of Major-Domo
13 Tannery
14 Soldiers' Quarters
15 Fountain
16 Basin for Washing Clothes
17 Part of Foundation of Second Church
18 Gardener's House
19 Indian Recreation Ground
20 Kilns
21 Aqueduct

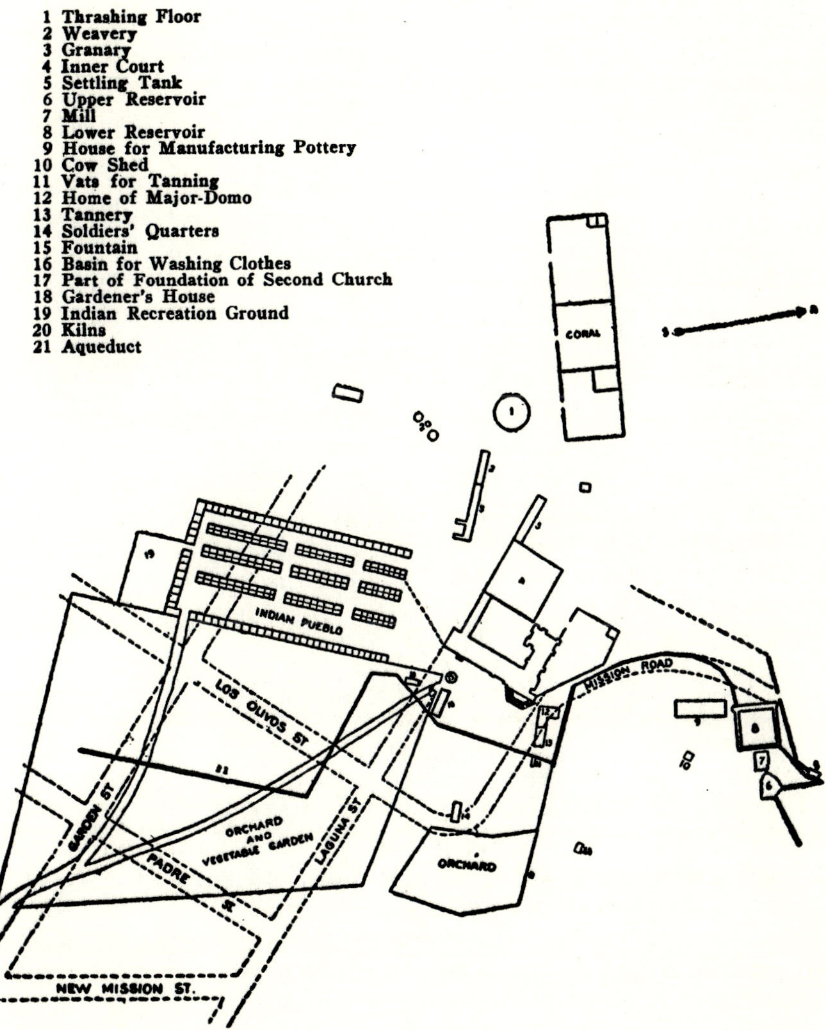

THE MISSION BUILDINGS AND GROUNDS AS THEY APPEARED IN 1840

in these rows had a breadth of about twelve feet and depth of thirty-one feet, each of the principal houses consisting of two rooms. A solid wall of adobe, nine feet high and crowned with tiles, surrounded the village; and against this wall, on the inside, were built other houses only one room in depth and with a breadth of about nineteen feet.

In 1798, the first nineteen houses were built. Two years later thirty-two more were built; and each succeeding year still more were added, until in 1807, two hundred and fifty-two had been erected. In 1804, a mud wall nine feet high was erected on the west side of the village, enclosing nearly an acre of ground, which was reserved for the use of the Indians. To-day, not one of the houses remains; but many of the stone foundations on which the houses rested could have been seen about a dozen years ago. Many square tiles were then visible half hidden under the turf; and here and there were large deposits of shells, which would indicate that shell fish was a staple article of diet at the Mission.

Although many of the Indians lived at the Mission, where they were employed, yet on account of the employment of others in cultivating the fields and in herding cattle, which required their being at a considerable distance from it, several rancherias were established where such Indians could live. One of the rancherias was on the Hope ranch, where the buildings of the Indians covered a considerable area, extending on both sides of Modoc road, a few hundred yards eastward from its intersection with Hollister Avenue. This locality was called the Cienegita, on account of the swampy land on the south side of the road; and on the western bank of the little creek which flows through the *cieniga* may still be seen some of the adobe ruins of the old buildings partly overgrown with tunas.

On account of the many Indians who lived at this rancheria an *asistencia,* as a small chapel under the control of a Mission was called, was built a few rods to the north of Modoc road. It was of adobe and had a breadth of twenty-seven feet and a depth of sixty-five feet. The music of a small organ and the voices of an Indian choir added to the interest of the services, which were attended not only by the natives but also by the early settlers of the valley. Although the Indians were scattered shortly after the secularization, yet, in the year 1860, the padres obtained a patent to an acre of land including the chapel and the adjoining graveyard. Services were held at the chapel until about ten years later. The tiles were then removed; the walls began to crumble; and now nothing remains but a few ruins.

While the padres gave much attention to their grain fields and cattle ranches, they also cultivated various kinds of fruit trees. The apple, pear, apricot, fig, and other trees were planted in an orchard which covered about three acres of land and which was situated one hundred yards in front of the Mission. It was surrounded by a six-sided wall that was strengthened by heavy buttresses of masonry. Part of the wall that extended along the northerly side is still in place, and hidden beneath sage brushes may still be seen the buttress that stood at the easterly corner. The fruit trees gradually died or were removed, until fifteen years ago there were only three standing. Now there is but one, which is still vigorous, though its bark is moss covered and its branches are much overgrown.

Another piece of land, of about sixteen acres in extent, adjoined the Indian village, and was laid out as a vegetable garden and olive orchard. It was surrounded by a wall of adobe, nine feet high, and covered with tiles which protected the upper part from rain. The most southerly corner of this wall was located about fifty feet southwest of Garden street and one hundred and fifty feet northwest of Mission street. The only trace of the wall that remains is part that extended along the southern side. In the southern quarter of the block bounded by Garden, Padre, Santa Barbara and Los Olivos streets, the stone foundations on which the wall rested appear above ground and may be traced for a hundred feet. But though the wall has disappeared, yet many of the old olive trees still live and cast their pleasing shade within the grounds of modern residences. In 1807, a house with a length of sixty feet and a depth of eighteen feet was built within this orchard, for the head gardener. It contained several apartments with a corridor in front, and was located a few rods from the south corner of the Mission buildings, near the spot where the large sycamore tree is now growing.

Passing along the Mountain Drive, half a mile beyond the Mission bridge, one will observe, to the east of the creek, a triangular shaped piece of land which has been cleared of the oaks which once grew there. This piece of land was the principal Mission vineyard and is still cultivated by the padres. Stone aqueducts pass along two of its sides, and near the northern corner was an adobe building where the tools were kept and the vintage was taken. Another vineyard was located at La Goleta, on the western bank of San Jose Creek, and nearly a mile north of Hollister Avenue. It consisted of seven and a half acres, and was surrounded on three sides by a willow fence and on the remaining side by the creek.

One of the principal occupations of the Indians not employed in the field was the tanning of hides, and in the year 1802, three vats were built for this purpose. They were constructed of bricks solidly joined with mortar, so as to form one solid piece of masonry, and were located two hundred and fifty feet directly east of the Mission church, where they can still be seen. In the same year was built the tannery, which had a length of sixty feet and a breadth of eighteen feet; and adjoining it on the northwest side was built the house of the major domo, which consisted of several rooms and a corridor. This latter building was close to the present church, and occupied the site where the home of Mr. Adair now stands. When the Mission road was widened, most of this building was torn down, but the adjacent tannery and the gardener's home were the last of the old buildings to be removed and were still standing in the year 1887.

During the first few years of the Mission's history, water for domestic and general use had been obtained with difficulty from the creek behind the Mission. But as the creek invariably dried up in the summer it was found necessary, in order to have an ample supply for the two thousand people who came to dwell at the Mission, and for the tanneries and gardens, to bring the water from the perennial springs of the canyon. It was also desirable to build a reservoir which would hold a quantity of water sufficient for general purposes during summer, in case of a drouth. This task was undertaken first, and in the year 1806, a large reservoir of masonry, one hundred and twenty-five feet square and with a depth of seven feet, was built upon the hillside, about five hundred feet from the Mission. It is the reservoir which is now used by the Santa Barbara Water Company for supplying the City of Santa Barbara.

THE THIRD DECADE AND LATER

In the year 1807, a large stone dam was built a mile and a half from the Mission, on the west fork of Pedregosa creek; and another dam was built about three miles from the Mission, on the east fork. Both of these dams are still in existence. The one on the left fork was used both to store the water and also to direct it to the aqueduct; but it is now so overgrown with brush as to be hardly noticeable. The one on the east fork was used solely as a weir for directing the water to the aqueduct.

It is filled to the upper level with gravel; but stands as firmly to-day as when constructed a century ago.

As it was found impracticable to make clay pipe for conducting the waters from the dams to the reservoir, pieces of stone were cut and chiseled so that when in place and cemented with mortar they formed aqueducts with conduits ten inches in depth and of the same breadth. These aqueducts were built so as to follow the contours of the hills and canyons from the dams to the reservoirs and so well were they constructed that after a hundred years they remain in excellent condition, excepting where they have been destroyed by man.

Subsequently a second reservoir of octagonal shape was built higher on the hill, and between it and the lower reservoir was the mill. Another aqueduct was then constructed leading from the dam, on the west fork of Mission creek, to the hill immediately north of the reservoir, whence it descended the steep slope of the hill to the upper reservoir. The latter shows signs of decay, yet displays the effective work of the early masons. A flight of stone steps leads down to the bottom where the debris of nearly a century has collected, and where a tree of fair proportions has taken root and grown several feet above the top of the reservoir. At the southern end is an opening, which was closed by a heavy oaken door when the water was not required to turn the water-wheel of the mill. The grooves where the door rose and descended may be plainly seen, and also the small holes in the upper part of the wall, where beams were erected, from which were suspended the pully and the rope used in raising the door. The mill is now in ruins. The threshing floor and space where the large water-wheel turned are still discernible; but the water wheel and the discs that ground the corn and wheat are gone.

One can not view the ruins without pictures of other days coming before the mind: the fertile valleys, turned golden brown with ripening grain; the Indians plodding homeward with the harvests; the water scurrying down the hill and splashing into the reservoir below; the creaking, groaning water-wheel; the slowly grinding discs; the Indians carrying the newly made flour to the storehouses; and watching and directing all, the brown-robed friars.

The water that was spent after passing through the mill flowed into the larger reservoir, which also received water from the lower stone aqueduct. This larger reservoir was used to store water for irrigation; and from its south corner an aqueduct followed the general course of the road to the church, whence crossing the road it passed along the wall of masonry which is still standing at the rear of the home of Mr. Adair, as far as the tannery. From this point the water was conducted to the small orchard for irrigation; but the main branch of the aqueduct passed through the large orchard, and a few years ago traces of it appeared where it crossed Garden street two hundred feet northwest of Padre street.

A short distance west of the upper reservoir is a small building of masonry that has been erroneously spoken of as a bathhouse. This building contained a settling tank where the water used for domestic purposes at the Mission was clarified. From this building the water was conducted to the rear of the Mission buildings in a cement pipe about four inches in diameter, which crossed along the top of a solid wall of masonry, part of which may still be seen, close to the present Mission bridge. At one time a beautiful arch in this wall of masonary spanned the road that crosses the bridge; but about the year 1880, as the opening in the wall was not sufficiently large to conveniently allow the passage of some of the farm wagons that constantly travelled that way, the arch and part of the wall were removed.

In the wall, separating the cemetery from the Mission road, was a gateway surmounted by a small stone cross. This entrance was closed with masonry many years ago, although the cross indicates where it was located.   A short distance from this former entrance and at a point where the aqueduct crosses the road, stands a living monument to kindhearted Father O'Keefe, one of the most beloved of the Mission padres.   In years gone by, he had observed some Indian women coming regularly to that spot and washing their clothes in the water that they took from the aqueduct. To protect them from the heat of the sun he planted four sycamores, two of which died.   The Indians have long since disappeared, yet two tall sycamores remain, and in their grateful shade many a weary person has sat and rested on the seat that reaches from trunk to trunk.

In the center of the inner court is a fountain, constructed of stone and covered with cement.   It was built in the year 1808, and is plain in appearance, being designed more for utility than for ornamentation. In front of the entrance to the cloister is a much larger fountain that was built at a later date.   It is of octagonal shape and is the handsomest of any of the Mission fountains, though it became somewhat defaced.   The top of the standard which rises from the center represents a pomegranate, and beneath it is a bowl, the sides of which were delicately carved; but the lime which in the course of nearly a century has been deposited from the waters which flowed over them has largely effaced the beauty of the original outlines.

From this fountain the water was formerly conducted into a large basin of masonry that is located immediately in front of it.   The stone head pieces, through which the water entered and issued from the basin, were designed to represent the heads of bears; but they have been so worn and broken that now they present but slight resemblance to those animals.   The basin has a length of sixty-five feet and a breadth of twenty-three feet.   Regularly once a week the women from the Indian village gathered there to wash their soiled clothes, which they scrubbed on the sloping sides of the basin where they knelt.

A short distance to the east of the lower stone reservoir, are the remains of a large building which was erected in the year 1808 for the manufacture of clay pipe and pottery. The former was used for conducting the water beneath the ground in places where an open aqueduct would be undesirable, and the latter was used for domestic purposes before the introduction of china ware. In the rooms of the Society of Natural History is a piece of pottery, made at the Mission and formerly owned by the writer, which bears much resemblance to the water pitchers used in the Orient. Very few pieces, however, of the Mission pottery now remain.

In the following year, an important improvement was begun in the Mission buildings, although it was not completed until 1811. Prior to 1809, the building adjoining the present church and on the ocean side of the square, contained the dwelling rooms of the priests and consisted of a row of rooms but a single tier in depth, in front of which was a corridor. When, however, on account of the increasing number of padres, more rooms were required, the corridor was removed and another tier of rooms was added, adjoining and in front of the first constructed tier. The front of the building was then finished with the arched corridor that exists to-day, the arches and pillars being constructed of solid masonry and the flooring paved with square tiles. The entrances to the newly constructed tier of rooms on the front were from the corridor; and the entrances to the tier of rooms, to the rear, were from the inner court. The building was then covered with a flat cement roof, but later, when the growing needs of the Mission required still more rooms, a second story was constructed above the present cloister.

A picture of the Mission taken in 1865, shows that previous to that time a second story had been added to only one-half of this part of the quadrangle; but subsequently the roof was raised along the whole length of this front, and more rooms were added.

At this period, traveling through Alta California was over trails, some of which were broad and well worn, but few of which attained to the dignity of roads, even after the introduction of the cumbersome ox-carts. Extending, however, along the coast from Mission to Mission was one well-traveled highway known as the Camino Real, or Royal Highway, which connected at San Diego with the system of Mission highways of Baja California, known as the Gulfo Camino, Sierra Camino, and Pacifico Camino. All of these highways were constructed by the padres as a means of communication between the Missions, and over them a mounted mail carrier bore the dispatches from the City of Mexico. The Camino Real was the road over which Junipero Serra regularly traveled when he visited the Missions which he had established in Alta California; and in later years it became the principal highway along the coast.

It would be impossible now to locate with absolute accuracy the course followed by the Camino Real throughout all its length. In fact, for short stretches, the route traveled must have varied slightly with the seasons. It was not concerned with government section lines nor neighbors' fences, but followed the course most convenient to travel from Mission to Mission. In the immediate vicinity of Santa Barbara, it is not probable that it followed the beach westward from the eastern limits of the city; as in those day, there would have been much difficulty, during many months of the year, in reaching either Mission or presidio from that di-

FORMER ARCH IN MISSION WALL

From an Etching by Henry Chapman Ford

The Mission of Santa Barbara in 1865

rection. The plat which accompanies the patent of the Pueblo of Santa Barbara, from the United States, in 1860, represents Mission creek emptying into the estero, which was then part of the lagoon. During heavy rains the creek forced its way to the ocean, and was difficult to cross; but after the heavy rains were over, the drifting beach sands barred the passage of the creek to the ocean, and the waters filled the estero. Later in the year when the creek ceased to flow in its lower stretches, the flowing springs of the De la Guerra Gardens fed the lake. Further eastward the old racetrack, recently bought by the city, was under water during winter, and the overflow from it, as well as the waters from Sycamore canyon, forced channels across the beach, where the yielding sands would make crossing dangerous.

The most direct route from Montecito to the Mission would have been to the north of the old racetrack and skirting the foothills; and during part of the year it would have been the only practical route. From a point near where Canon Perdido street reaches the base of the foothills, a branch road probably passed around the head of the lagoon to the presidio.

Westward from the Mission, the Camino Real undoubtedly followed the general direction of Hollister Avenue; yet for the first three or four miles it probably turned a little more to the south, and passed along the low rolling hills, so as to avoid the little lagoons and lands which in winter are heavy and soggy. The rancheria of Hope ranch as well as the chapel, which were south of Hollister Avenue, would also have diverted the road in that direction.

It was never a paved highway like some of the *Caminos Reales of Mexico.* It was little more than a broad trail, often leading between thickets of shrubs and under branches of oaks, or on the high banks bordering the ocean; yet it is of greater historic interest, today, than any other road in California.

The severe earthquakes which occurred at Santa Barbara in December, 1812, and during the following three months, did great damage to many of the Mission buildings; and the walls of the adobe church were injured to such an extent, that it was decided to remove the church and build a new one. A couple of years were required to repair the buildings which had been injured and to remove the ruins of the old church; but in the year 1815, the foundation of the present one was laid. All of the other buildings of the Mission were of adobe; but in order to construct a building that would resist the force of future earthquakes, the walls were built of cubes of sandstone, firmly cemented with mortar. They had a thickness of six feet, and were supported by heavy buttresses, so that the church is the most strongly built of any Mission in California. On account of the length of the rafters, it was found impractical to bring them from the San Rafael Mountains, where the Indians had cut most of the timbers previously used in the Mission buildings; and a vessel was accordingly sent to Santa Cruz Island to obtain them. The roof was covered with tiles; and the crude bitumen was melted and laid for a flooring.

Exclusive of the buttress but including the walls, the extreme length of the church is one hundred and seventy-eight feet and the width is thirty-nine feet. The length of the nave exclusive of the choir is one hundred and thirty-eight feet and the breadth between the walls is twenty-seven feet. Of the six chapels, the two nearest the entrance are built in the solid walls that are of double thickness at these points. Within a recess in the pediment above the entrance is a carved figure of painted stone representing Santa Barbara; and resting above the cornice at each end are two other statues of stone, which with a third, that has been removed, represented the cardinal virtues, Faith, Hope, and Charity.

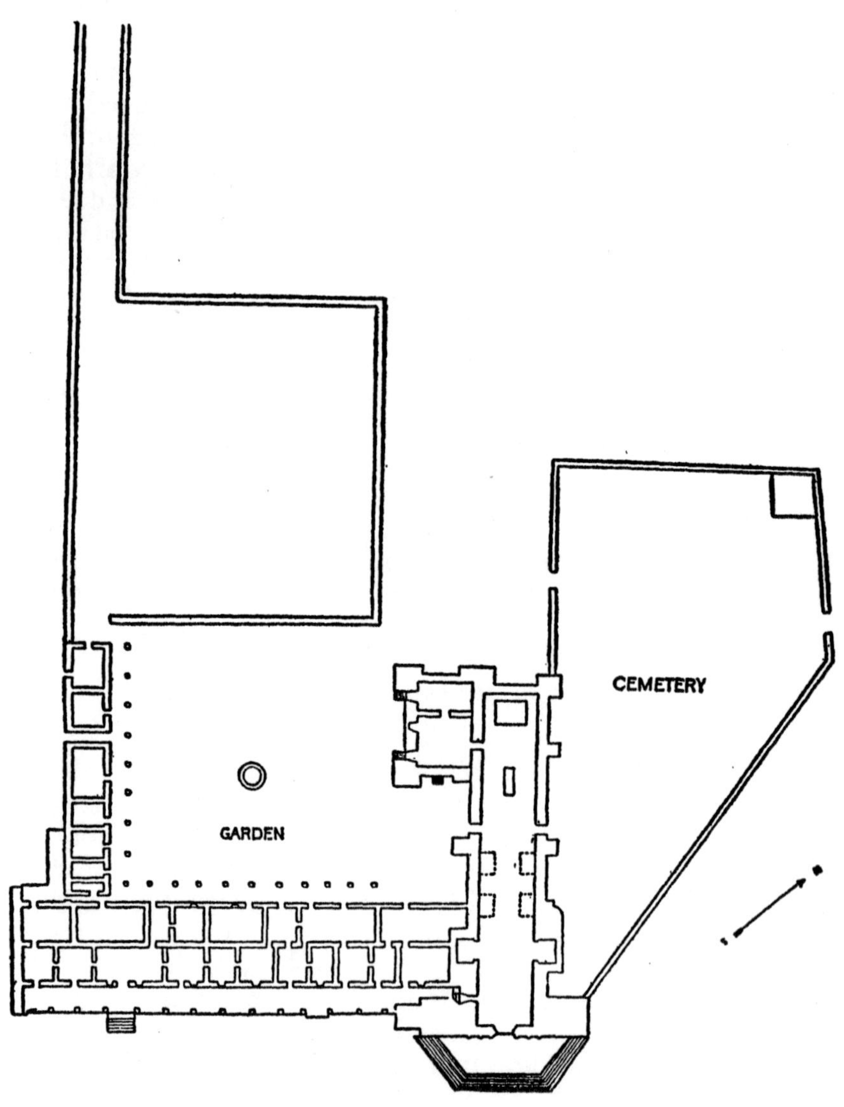

GROUND PLAN OF THE MISSION CHURCH IN 1890

The tower, on the left, that is approached by winding stone steps from the corridor has always been the principal belfry, and at one time contained six bells, all of which were of brass. The two largest bells weigh eight hundred and twenty-five and five hundred and seventy pounds, respectively, and were cast in the year 1808, by Manuel Vargas. They are silent now, but their ragged edges speak eloquently of the past. Some of the smaller bells are older, and on one that bears the inscription "AVE, MARIA, PURISSIMA, SANTA BARBARA," is the date, 1804, and on another is the date 1797.

At the right of the high altar is a tomb where are buried the remains of the first bishop of California, Fr. Francisco Garcia Diego y Moreno. In the basement beneath the nave of the church are the remains of Governor Figueroa, who died in 1833, and here also are buried the remains of Don Jose De la Guerra and his son, Don Pablo De la Guerra. In the Mission churchyard are buried a number of persons prominent in the early life of Santa Barbara; while in trenches, between parallel rows of masonry, the tops of which appear at the surface of the ground, are the remains of some five thousand Indians who belonged to the Mission settlement.

In the early days, the Indians were required to regularly attend the services held in the Mission church. There was an Indian choir and also an Indian orchestra of thirty musicians who played violins, flutes, drums, and trumpets. This orchestra was instructed by Father Duran, who was an enthusiastic conductor; and, not infrequently, the services were enlivened by strains of dance music, interpolated with the more solemn anthems.

In the Mission life, few exciting or unusual events occurred, but in 1824, a concerted outbreak among the Indians of several of the Missions of the Coast caused

great excitement among the Indians resident at Santa
Barbara. The conspiracy originated among the Indians of the Missions of La Purissima and Santa Ynez,
and word was conveyed from them to the Indians of the
Missions of San Luis Obispo, Santa Barbara, San
Buenaventura, and San Fernando, to prepare for an uprising on the 22nd of February. The plans were prepared with such secrecy that the padres had no intima-
tion of the approaching danger; and Jose De la Guerra
seems to have been the only one of the class called *gente
de razon,* or people of enlightenment, who had any sus-
picion of the uprising. An Indian woman, employed
in his family, intimated to him that she had heard of the
threatened attack, but for so many years had the Indians
submitted unresistingly that he placed little confidence
in her story.

On the evening of the 21st, the Indians of the Santa
Ynez Mission made an attack on the padres residing
there, and on the following day several of the leaders
of the Santa Barbara Indians excited the others, by re-
hearsing grievances of the past. Watching their opportunity, they seized some guns, and with these and with
their bows and arrows wounded two of the soldiers who
were stationed as a guard at the Mission. Captain De
la Guerra was summoned, and he at once marched from
the presidio with a force of soldiers. In the fight which
occurred the Indians had the advantage of being protected by the walls of the buildings and wounded four
of the soldiers; but two of their own number were killed
and three wounded. The Indians then retreated, with
such property as they could carry, to the foothills of the
mountains, and after a few days crossed to the lower
part of the San Joaquin Valley. They were pursued
thither by the soldiers; and one or two engagements occurred, in which several were killed or wounded, on
each side; finally, however, a full pardon being prom-

ised the Indians, they returned peacefully to the Mission.

The Mission church of Santa Barbara is, to-day, the best preserved and handsomest of all the Missions of California. In the presence of the colossal cathedrals of the world, the crowning works of master hands, the beholder stands in awestriken admiration. But there is nothing in either the external or internal structure of the Mission to evoke such feelings of wondering admiration; yet as the eye of the visitor passes over the church, unpretentious in its simplicity; looks out into the church yard and over the hills with their crumbling ruins; and the mind recalls the many vicissitudes of the first years of the Mission life; there is awakened a feeling of warm attachment to this old church and to all that has been associated with it, such as few of the more costly temples can inspire.

THE SECULARIZATION

THE secularization of the Missions presents one of the saddest pictures in the history of the state of California. For half a century, the padres had toiled with unremitting zeal to Christianize the Indians and teach them the arts of civilization. Under their influence the hills had been made to teem with cattle, the valleys to produce harvests, and the vineyards and orchards to bear their fruits. In every large valley of the southern coast rose the tower of a Mission church, and near at hand were the Indian dwellings, the shops of native artisans, and the storehouses. Trade had become established between these Mission outposts and the cities of the east. Settlers came to dwell among them, and the birth of a new nation on the shores of the Pacific was made known to the world. Yet their system, under which the Indians were reduced to a condition of dependance and large areas of land were controlled by the church, was unfavorable to the political and commercial progress of the country and was consequently overthrown. The transition from the glory of the Missions to their ruin was sudden and complete. The Mission bells ceased to toll; the walls crumbled to decay; and the Indians, half-clothed and half-fed, returned again to their native state and soon disappeared. Yet the work of the padres should not be undervalued as they were the pioneer settlers of the coast.

Nearly a century before the founding af the first Mission in Alta California, Father Juan Maria Salvatierra undertook to found the Missions of Baja California. To accomplish this purpose, those piously inclined of Spain and Mexico were induced to grant or bequeath sums of money to be used for the conversion of the benighted natives of the two Californias. Some of those gifts and bequests amounted to many thousand pesos, and in the course of a few years the aggregate became very large and was known as the *Fundo Piedoso de California* or the Pious Fund. This fund was carefully invested by the Jesuits and rapidly increased in value. When the Jesuits were expelled from the Missions and the Franciscans given control, the latter enjoyed every privilege exercised by the former, in using the income derived from the Pious Fund. With this income the Missions of Alta California were built; and from the cattle furnished by the Missions of Baja California the vast herds belonging to the Missions of Alta California sprung. It would, therefore, appear that the padres had not only a prescriptive right to the lands they had occupied and cultivated, but also a legal right to the herds of cattle and the buildings.

But the Mexican government regarded the Mission rights very differently and claimed that the best interests of the Indians demanded that they be allowed full liberty and given land on which to support themselves. Accordingly, in 1833, the Mexican Congress decreed that the Missions should be converted into parishes and the padres should be superceded by secular curates. It was also decreed that all expenses connected with the secularization of the Missions should be paid for out of the Pious Fund. The territorial deputation was in harmony with the ideas of the Mexican Congress, and on July 31, 1834, they adopted the plan which, when carried out, resulted in complete secularization of the Missions, although several years elapsed before their ruin was accomplished.

The salient features of the plan were that the missionaries, until replaced by the new curates, should be limited in their duties to administrating to the spiritual needs of the Indians, while the secular possessions should be under the care of the government; that the missionary property should be limited to the church and a building for the residence of the curate; and that the other buildings and property should be converted to such ends as the government might desire. Part of the lands were set aside as districts which were divided into sections to be allotted among the Indians. The lands, however, were not mortgageable, nor could perfect title be obtained, until after several years of occupation. One-half of the grain, cattle, and implements, belonging to the Missions, was to be divided among the Indians.

Major-domos were chosen to take charge of the Mission property, and commissioners were appointed to make inventories. To a large extent, the plan was carried out as it had been projected, but in most instances it proved an utter failure. As soon as at liberty, most of the Indians refused to work and many of them took to the mountains; others who attempted to cultivate the ground were so harassed by the whites that their lot became unendurable. The restraint to which they had been subjected for a couple of generations had enervated as well as elevated, and in a few years they almost entirely disappeared. At last, realizing their mistake, the government made several ineffectual efforts to regain the confidence of the Indians, but it was too late. Not only was the plan a failure in its design of elevating them by emancipation, but it resulted in the most wanton waste and fraud. The duties of the Commissioners, Major-domos, and other officers, connected with the secularization, admitted of numerous opportunities for peculations. Nearly all of the Missions were soon desolate and in ruins; but as the large majority of the people of influence in California were interested in the change, there was no one to interfere but the missionaries, whose voices were raised in vain.

Owing to the many disturbances of this period, regular statistics were not kept at the Santa Barbara Mission later than 1834, and many interesting events doubtless passed unrecorded. The Mission of Santa Barbara probably suffered less than any other; for while it lost most of its secular possessions, and many of its buildings were allowed to fall to decay, yet the church and the cloisters were well preserved. One reason for this was the fact that the padres were natives of Mexico and not Spaniards; and, consequently one of the principal grounds of hostility was removed. But still another reason existed. In 1839, a new diocese was created of Alta California, and Father Francisco Garcia Diego y Moreno was appointed bishop. He chose Santa Barbara as his episcopal see, and as he made his home at the Mission he undoubtedly had great influence in its being well preserved.

It had been decreed by the Mexican Congress of 1836 that the Pious Fund, which at that time amounted to about two million of dollars, and had practically been confiscated by the government, should be entrusted to the bishop, when appointed. Relying upon this resource, the bishop at once planned to found a theological school and monastery at Santa Barbara, and also to build a cathedral. Work had already progressed to the extent of collecting rock for the foundations of the different buildings, when news was received that Santa Ana, who was then in power, had declined to recognize the bishop's right to the fund, and that most of it had been converted into money and paid into the public treasury. The work was accordingly abandoned, and Santa Barbara lost a Catholic cathedral.

An effort was finally made, in 1843, for the restoration of the old Mission system, but the change came too late. The conditions, under which the Mission system could exist, had been swept away, and nothing could restore it. Nearly all the Mission properties were in debt, and their incomes had ceased to be sufficient for the maintenance of both public worship and the care of the Indians. The latter were in a most deplorable condition and, in many cases, were actually suffering the pangs of hunger. Finally on October 28, 1845, a proclamation was made for the sale of nine of the Missions; and others, including Santa Barbara, were leased for a term of years. The property of the Santa Barbara Mission was leased to Nicholas A. Den and Daniel Hill for the yearly rental of $1200.00, the part leased consisting of all the storerooms and other buildings of the Mission, with the exception of the church and the cloister. The San Marcos rancho and some fifteen hundred head of horses and cattle and seventeen hundred head of sheep, belonging to the Mission property, were leased also, The bishop, at last, realized the impossibility of checking the work of ruin that was taking place about him; and his death was probably hastened by his disappointment. In 1846, he died, and was buried in the Mission church at Santa Barbara.

The Missions of California played a most important part in the early development of the state, as each formed a nucleus, about which in time sprang up towns and cities. But the Mexican independence which resulted at the end of the war with Spain, in 1821, and the liberty of action and freedom of thought which followed, sounded the death knell to their existence. It was impossible that their system of land tenure could obtain with the growth of population under a republican government. Although it may be said of the secularization that it was necessary that it should be done, yet it was not done wisely. There were undoubtedly some abuses and some mistreatment of the Indians, as charged; nevertheless, abuses have been incidental to all governments, and no one will question the fact that among the padres of the California Missions were some of the most ingenious, self-sacrificing men California has known. With no thought of personal gain, but devoted to a sacred cause, they endured every hardship,

braved every danger.   Though the names of most of
them are forgotten, yet the name of one, now sleeping
beneath the Mission at Monterey, should be remembered for centuries to come; for ecclesiastical history
presents the names of few men who can be regarded as
more useful, more noble, than Junipero Serra.

Though the bells of the Mission towers be silent;
though the walls crack and crumble; all that remains
should be held sacred; for the Missions are the oldest
antiquities of California; they represent the efforts of
manly character and noble purposes; and are dedicated
to the Christian religion.

THE PUEBLO

THE settlement of the Spaniards on this coast resulted in four distinct lines of growth—the presidio, the Mission, the pueblo, and the rancho.

The pueblo was the outgrowth of the presidio, and virtually began to exist soon after the latter was established; although the first town council was not elected until December, 1826. The soldiers who married and wished to remain at Santa Barbara, after their terms of service had expired, were allotted lands without the presidio walls for homes. Their descendants also built homes in the pueblo; and as years passed, others from Mexico, Spain, and France settled here. To the names of the comandantes might be added those of Cota, Gutierrez, Ruiz, Arrellanes, Lataillade, Jansens, Aguirre; as the names of a few who were well known in the early days of Santa Barbara. There were also a number of Anglo-Saxons, who came during the early part of the last century, and who subsequently became prominent in the life of the pueblo and the County of Santa Barbara. One of the earliest of these arrivals was Daniel Hill, a native of Massachusetts, who came to the coast in the year 1822, as captain of a trading vessel en route to the Hawaiian Islands. In the following year he settled at Santa Barbara, and six years later he was naturalized. After being engaged as a merchant for several years, and occasionally acting as carpenter and mason, he turned his atention to ranching and acquired extensive lands about Goleta.

Alpheus B. Thompson, who was interested in a fleet of ships engaged in collecting and transporting hides to Boston, also settled at Santa Barbara, about the same time; and marrying the daughter of Comandante Carrillo, became identified with the social and business life of the pueblo.

In 1829, Alfred Robinson arrived from Boston on the *Brookline,* which was one of the vessels engaged in the Pacific coast trade. He was agent of the owners of the fleet for the purchase of hides, and for twelve years resided on this coast. Part of this time he spent in Santa Barbara, where he met and married Anna Maria Antonia, the beautiful daughter of Captain De la Guerra. At the time of her marriage, she was but fourteen years of age; and the wedding was celebrated with festivities which lasted three or four days, and in which all the residents of the pueblo participated. In his book, entitled "Life in California," Mr. Robinson has left us a most interesting description of life on this coast at the period when he lived here.

Formerly large numbers of otter existed in the waters of Santa Barbara Channel, and as their skins were of a finer quality than the skins of those found elsewhere on the coast, they were hunted persistently by both Russians and Americans. Among the latter was Louis F. Burton, who arrived in 1831 and subsequently married Antonia Carrillo. He was a well-known hunter and trapper, and for years lived in a picturesque adobe overlooking the ocean from the crest of Burton's Mound, which was named after him.

George Nidever, a native of Tennessee, was another hunter and trapper who arrived in the early thirties, after crossing the Rocky Mountains with the Walker party. He was at one time a member of the famous little band called Graham's Riflemen, which took part in some of the early Californian revolutions. Like many of the pioneers, he was a remarkable rifle shot, and is reported to have killed some two hundred grizzlies and on one occasion to have shot three rifle bullets into a piece of paper that was one inch square and was placed at a distance of sixty yards. In 1853, he rescued the old

Indian woman from San Nicholas Island. His home for many years was on the Nidever property that was located near the eastern end of the present ocean boulevard.

Nicholas A. Den, an Irish physician, arrived in 1836, and shortly afterwards married the daughter of Daniel Hill. Although highly educated and accustomed to the life of cities, yet the ranch life appealed to him so strongly that he settled here permanently, and before his death had become the owner of the Dos Pueblos, Canada del Corral, San Marcos and Tequespis ranches, as well as ten thousand head of cattle.

Benjamin Fox, an English sailor, settled here in 1837, and at first engaged in the mercantile business, but later turned his attention to stock raising and became the owner of the Tinacquaic ranch.

There were but few distinct occupations in which the settlers engaged. As the country was well suited to ranching, many of the Mexicans and most of the Americans, although living in the pueblo where they could enjoy its social life, owned large tracts of land on which they raised cattle for the hides and tallow. A few Americans, who lived by hunting and trapping, and had reached this part of the coast after years spent on the plains and in the Rocky Mountains, found congenial employment in hunting the otter. A number of Mexicans acquired small patches of fertile land, where the canyons opened into the valleys, and building ditches to irrigate their lands, raised vegetables and fruits which they sold. Two or three Americans, agents for the coasting vessels, were employed in purchasing and shipping hides and tallow. Other residents were merchants; but there was no business center in the pueblo, nor were there any business blocks. The store of the merchant was connected with his home, and was simply a large outside room where groceries and dry-goods, as well as tobacco and liquors, could be bought or exchanged for other commodities. Although the growth of the pueblo was slow, yet, in 1830, it had a population of approximately four hundred, of whom about ten were foreigners; and consisted of sixty houses which were built without any regard to streets, as the first owners of the land chose lots where it seemed most convenient.

It is uncertain when the first formal grant of pueblo land was made to any resident, but the earliest deed recorded was one dated the 14th of February, 1835; and was a grant to Octaviano Gutierrez of a piece of land to be used as a homestead, and consisting of one hundred varas square, located between the presidio and the Mission.

All the houses were of adobe with a foundation of stone; and nearly all had tiled roofs. As timber was scarce many of the houses had no other flooring than the ground; a few of them had a flooring of asphalt; and the first house with a wooden flooring is said to have been one built by Daniel Hill about the year 1824. Most of the houses were of simple structure, like the small adobes still remaining in parts of the city; but there were a few which deserve special mention.

Probably the first house of any consequence which was built without the walls of the presidio, is one known as the Arrellanes house; and which is located three or four rods from where the most easterly corner of the presidio wall formerly stood. Part of it was built by a Spaniard about the year 1795, and additions have been made from time to time to meet the requirements of the different owners. As the walls of these additions have different thicknesses, some being about three feet thick, and others about a foot less, it can readily be determined what rooms were added at different periods. For many years one part of the building was used as a residence, and another part was used as a store for the sale of general merchandise and

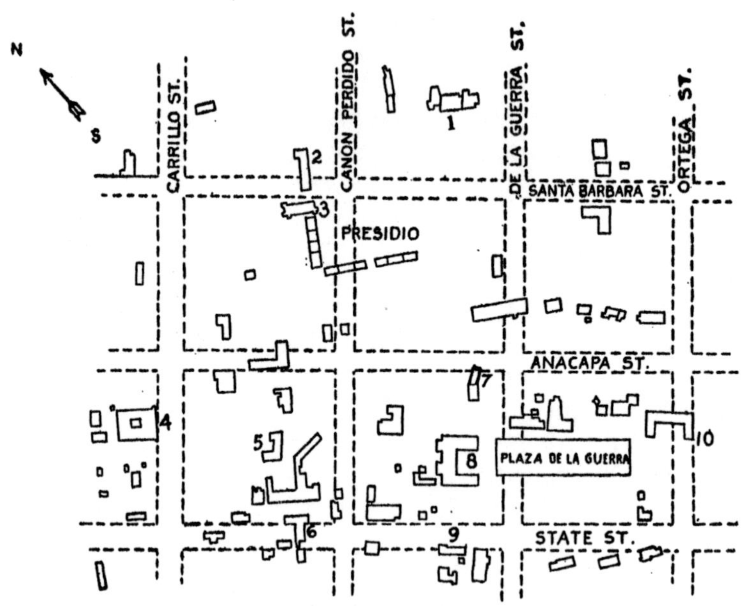

PUEBLO OF SANTA BARBARA

1, Teodoro Arrellanes. 2, Gumesindo Flores. 3, Church. 4, Jose Aguirre. 5, Raimundo Carrillo. 6, Louis Burton. 7, Gaspar   Orena. 8, Jose De la Guerra. 9, Alpheus Thompson (St. Charles Hotel). 10, Carlos Carrillo.

liquors. Finally the ownership passed to Teodoro Arrellanes, whose family and descendants have lived there for over two generations.

The only two-story house in the pueblo, excepting the small structure erected at the rear of the De la Guerra house, was the one now known as the former St. Charles hotel which is located on State street near De la Guerra. It was built about the year 1835 by Alpheus B. Thompson, who lived there for many years, while engaged in the shipping business. Several changes have been made in the arrangement of its rooms, and its external appearance is somewhat different now from what it was formerly; as then the approach to the upper story was by an open staircase, constructed on the southeast side of the building.

Almost opposite the public library on Carrillo street, was the Aguirre house, which was considered by many the most attractive home in old Santa Barbara. It was built in the year 1841, by Jose Antonio Aguirre, a native of San Sebastian, Spain, who, after visiting Mexico and South America, became a merchant and trader on this coast. In his own vessel he brought some of the material with which it was embellished; and skilled artisans were employed in the construction. It was a large one-story house with a score of apartments, and was built of adobe with foundations that elevated it a few feet above the ground. The square front was relieved by a veranda, the roof of which was supported by curved columns. The parlor was a large and handsomely finished room, with floors of polished hard wood and with walls daintily frescoed. Luxurious sofas, chairs of mahogany, and paintings of rare workmanship, furnished and adorned the rooms. But the most unique feature, built in imitation of the architecture of Spain and Mexico, was the inner court, or *patio,* that was paved with stone and surrounded by a corridor with a wooden floor. Handsomely hand-carved posts supported the roof of the corridor, which was so constructed as to leave a circular opening above the stone pavement.. In the retirement of this inner court, open to the air, the family could live during the warm months of the year; and to further add to their privacy a stone wall was built surrounding the orchard and flower gardens. La Casa de Aguirre, as it was known, was a favorite place for holding fiestas, in the olden days, and it was one of the most popular homes in Santa Barbara.

The Comandante's house, in the presidio, was necessarily a very important house when California was under the Spanish and Mexican rule, as here the official receptions were held. Unfortunately the laying out of Santa Barbara street necessitated the removal of part of the house, and its attractiveness has still further been lessened by the erection of a small house in front of it; but formerly it was the most noticeable structure in the presidio, with the exception of the church. Gumesindo Flores was the last comandante to live there, and his descendants still make it their home.

There were other interesting houses in the pueblo, but those who came here in the early days relate that the one of most imposing appearance was the De la Guerra house, the construction of which was begun about the year 1819 and finished in 1826. Originally, it was slightly different from what it is now. Then the corridors extended about the three sides of the patio for the full length of each side, and heavy columns, each of which were made of flat tiles, twenty inches square and placed one upon another, supported a tiled roof. Subsequently, additional dwelling rooms were constructed at each end of the corridor; and the red tiled columns were unfortunately broken by an earthquake and replaced by wooden posts. The appartments of the house were spacious, and many of the furnishings were brought from Spain. In the garden, to the rear, was a small two story building made of adobe, the upper story of which was once used as the library. Adjoining the passage that leads from the front corridor to the garden was the *bodega,* where the lord of two hundred thousand acres kept the choice wines he poured to the health of his countless guests. As the residence of Captain De la Guerra, comandante of the presidio and one of the most influential citizens in Alta California, and of his son Don Pablo, state senator and lieutenant governor of the state, it acquired almost official prominence. It was also known as the home of Senora Noriega, whose goodness was proverbial; and the beauty and grace of its women, who were famed throughout California, made it the center of the social life of the pueblo.

Seventy-five years ago, the pueblo of Santa Barbara was one of a small group of settlements, widely scattered along the coast of southern California. It was nearly two thousand miles distant from any city of importance, and was separated from the mother country by a great continent and ocean that then took many months to cross. A large percentage of its inhabitants were descendants of Spaniards who had intermarried with the natives of Mexico and were deficient in higher education; yet there existed in the social life of the people a refinement which, under the circumstances, is almost surprising and which is one of the highest tributes to the influence of the Mission padres and the few influential families who created and maintained the standard. In the homes of the best people of this little pueblo existed the dignity, elegance, refinement, and charm of people reared in the capitals of the old world. Although the environment was not such as would stimulate intellectual effort, yet the people lived in an atmosphere of gentleness and grace, which affected all classes.

Both men and women were fond of dress; and laces, silks, kid gloves, silk stockings, and dainty slippers were

worn on proper occasions.   An American who saw
Santa Barbara about 1840 referred to the dress of a
daughter of Don Jose de la Guerra, on the occasion of
her visiting a ship, which had arrived in the harbor,
and stated that "she wore pink silk stockings and the
daintiest little red slippers with silver buckles."

Mr. Robinson has left the following description of
the dress of the people of Santa Barbara at the time he
lived here.

"The dress worn by the middling class of females is
a chemise with short embroidered sleeves, richly
trimmed with lace, a muslin petticoat, flounced with
scarlet and secured at the waist by a silk band of the
same color, shoes of velvet or blue satin, a cotton *reboso,*
or scarf, pearl necklace and ear-rings, with the hair
falling in broad plaits down the back. Others of the
higher class dress in the English style, and instead of
the reboso substitute a rich and costly shawl of silk or
satin. There is something graceful in the management
of the reboso that the natives alone can impart, and the
perfect nonchalance with which it is thrown about them
and worn adds greatly to its beauty.

"Very few of the men have adopted our mode of
dress, the greater part adhering to the ancient costume
of the past century. Short clothes, and jacket trimmed
with scarlet, a sash about the waist, *botas* of ornamental
and embroidered deerskin, secured by colored garters,
embroidered shoes, the hair long, braided and fastened
behind with ribbons, a black silk handkerchief around
the head, surmounted by an oval and broad-brimmed
hat, is the dress universally worn by the men of California."

But if they loved fine clothes, which certainly became
them, their hearts were kind and simple. "My house
is your home, senor," was the greeting to the stranger
who knocked unexpectedly at the door. From the City
of Mexico to the pueblo of San Francisco a stranger

House of the Comandante

could travel without a *peso* in his pocket. Wherever he knocked at night, the door was opened. The best room in the house, a place at the fireside and the table, and in the morning a fresh horse for his journey, if his own was jaded—all were his, and to offer recompense was to offer insult. It is not surprising that such simple-minded, big-hearted people soon parted with their lands.

There were no finer horsemen in the world; and one of their greatest sports was to ride at full speed, and then stop within a few feet of a given line, by suddenly reining the horse on his haunches; or to gallop at full speed and, without checking the horse, pick up from the ground a sombrero or silver dollar; or to grasp the greased head of a rooster, the body of which was buried in the sand, and lift it from the ground. The common mode of travel was by horseback, the men being constantly in the saddle; and although women occasionally rode mounted alone, yet they generally rode seated behind their husbands or brothers. Carriages were almost unknown in California before 1845, although Santa Barbara was particularly fortunate in the ownership of two, one of which was the property of the Mission, and the other the property of Captain De la Guerra. But there were a number of springless ox-carts, with their lumbering wheels of solid oak, and slow plodding oxen; and when used as family conveyances they were furnished with leather coverings and cushions.

These were a peace-loving, pleasure-loving people; and they enjoyed many festive days. Near the junction of Garden and Cota streets was located what is known as the De la Guerra Gardens, formerly the private property of that family, and where fruit and vegetables were grown for their private use. But the shady trees which grew there luxuriously and the many springs of water made them an attractive pleasure ground, to which the friends of the family, who included all the good people of the pueblo, were frequently invited to celebrate some holiday. The three days' festivity which celebrated the wedding of Mr. Alfred Robinson in 1836, and which was spoken of by Mr. Dana in his "Two years before the Mast," was but one of the many recurring occasions of general pleasure-making and re-joicing.

The following account by Mr. Alfred Robinson of the wedding of Don Manuel Jimineo with Dona Maria de las Angustias De la Guerra, which occurred in 1837, gives an excellent idea of some of the customs prevailing in the pueblo at that time:

"On the marriage eve the bride went with her father to the Mission dressed in her usual church costume, which was deep black; where the joining of hands took place towards morning, and at a late hour the church ceremonies were performed. Breakfast was served with considerable taste, a task to which the worthy friar was fully competent. At the conclusion the bride and bridegroom were escorted to the house of her father. Padre Antonio had made his Indians happy by distributing presents among them; and many of the younger ones, well attired for the occasion, joined in the procession. They approached the town without any regular order until arriving almost within its pre-cincts; where under the direction of the friar, they formed and marched in the following manner: First came the military band, consisting of about twenty per-formers, who were dressed in a new uniform of red jackets trimmed with yellow cord, with pantaloons made after the Turkish fashion, and red caps of the Polish order. Then followed the bride and bride-groom, in an open English barouche, accompanied by the sister of the former. After these in a close carriage came Don Jose and Father Antonio; in another the *Madrina* and cousins, and lastly numbers of men and women on horseback. Guns were fired alternately, at the Mission and in the presidio until their arrival at the house of the 'fiesta de boda.' At one o'clock a large number of invited guests sat down at a long table, to partake of an excellent dinner. The married couple were seated at the head with the father spiritual on the right; and the father temporal on the left. Dinner being over, part of the company retired to their homes, whilst some of the younger members adjourned to a booth, which was prepared in the court yard, sufficiently large to contain several hundred people. Here they danced a while and then retired. Early in the evening, people, invited and uninvited, began to fill up the booth, and soon dancing commenced. The music consisted of two violins and a guitar, on which were performed many beautiful waltzes and contra-dances, together with a number of local melodies. During the evening all took active part in the amusement, and as the poorer classes exhibited their graceful performances, the two fathers from an elevated position threw at their feet silver dollars, and donations. The 'Fandango' lasted until the morning light appeared, accompanied with all the variety customary on such occasions.

"On the next day, Father Antonio as a further compliment to the bride, had dinner prepared in the corridor of the Mission, the table reaching from one end to the other, and the place being adorned with flags. Here all the town was invited to participate, where old and young, rich and poor, lame and blind, black and white, joined in the feast. For several succeeding nights the 'Fandango' was repeated at the booth, and they had enough of feasting and dancing intermingled with the amusements of the 'Carnes toleridas' to last them for some time."

Few of the festivities were regarded as being sufficiently important to be recorded; but an event long remembered was the coming of Bishop Garcia Diego to make Santa Barbara his official residence. The whole population of the pueblo prepared to welcome the first bishop of California; and as the vessel which brought him from the south came to anchor, every house was deserted; and men, women, and children gathered on the beach and on bended knees received his blessing. The guns of the presidio proclaimed the welcome, as the soldiers with beating drums and flowing banners escorted the bishop, who seated in a carriage passed beneath triumphal arches, which had been made by the women. After he had partaken of refreshments at the home of one of the leading families, the rejoicing people led him to his carriage, from which they had removed the horses; and forming in procession dragged it to the Mission.

Within nearly every house was a guitar, and when evening came and twilight darkened, from all parts of the pueblo were heard the sounds of music and rich melodious voices. There was something distinctly characteristic in their songs, in most of which there was a minor tone of sweet plaintiveness. When the lamps were hung and the guitars and violins sounded the waltz, light hearts beat and merry peals of laughter floated through the old California homes. Lissom forms glided gracefully through the halls. Dark velvety eyes looked words unspoken. The hours passed rapidly by, and before the last dance had been stepped and the last soft glance given, the bells of the old Mission tower had sounded the matin call. Those were halcyon days in the fairest spot in a lotus land.

THE RANCHOS

WHEN the Mission was established, it acquired possession of large tracts of land that were necessary for supporting the Mission settlement. Some of this land was segregated as ranches to be used for different purposes; as for instance: the lands tributary to El Capitan were at first used exclusively for raising sheep; and the Rancho San Julian was for several years leased by the Mission to the presidio for raising beef. At the time of the secularization these different ranches passed to different owners. There were, however, many valuable tracts of land that the Mission never made use of; and these the Mexican government granted to prominent men of the early days, as a reward for services to the state. In this way much of the valuable land of Santa Barbara County was granted away. Some of the grants comprise as many as forty thousand acres, and in all there were about thirty grants of ranches in the present county.

In a fertile valley on each ranch sprang up the ranch settlement, consisting of the homes of the owner, the dwellings where the major-domo and the vaqueros lived, and the sheds and corrals for the horses. All of the buildings were of adobe; and often were picturesquely located by some stream of water, beneath the shade of oaks. About others were planted the pepper trees so characteristic of Southern California, and which seem to have been introduced by the padres who brought them from Mexico. Every ranch home of importance had its vegetable garden, vinyard, and orchard. The principal grape grown was a dark purple one, now known as the Mission grape; and in the orchards were raised citrons , lemons, oranges, pomegranites, figs, peaches, apples, and pears.

With the exception of a few acres near the setlement, very little of the ground was cultivated. This was probably due to the lack of suitable implements, as the only plows in use were made of crooked branches of a tree. To one end of the branch was sometimes attached a sharpened piece of iron; and the other end was fastened to the horns of the oxen. But if only a small part of he land was cultivated, over the hills roamed large bands of horses and herds of cattle, which a few vacqueros on their horses were constantly following and rounding up, as there were no fences in those days. Horses multiplied so rapidly that they were regarded as of little value; and large bands of unclaimed horses roamed wild over the county, consuming pasturage which was needed for the cattle. Accordingly, they were frequently driven into corrals where they were killed by a well-directed spear thrust. Even as early as 1815, they were regarded as being of such detriment that at Santa Barbara a wholesale slaughter of horses was made that year.

Probably none of the ranches of Santa Barbara County was granted prior to the year 1800, but one of the earliest grants was that of the Rancho del Refugio, which was granted to Captain Jose Francisco Ortega about that time. The ownership of this ranch passed to his son, Don Jose Maria Ortega, known as Sergeant Ortega, under whose care it was developed and improved, until it presented the appearance of a little Mission. There were numerous houses at the main settlement, which was located near the ocean about thirty miles up the coast from Santa Barbara; and in the picturesque canyon not far from the ocean was erected a mill for grinding the corn. Higher up the canyon was a dam and an aqueduct for directing the water to the mill and thence conducting it to the orchards and vegetable gardens. The Ortegas were noted for their hospitality; and all who passed up or down the

The De La Guerra House

coast were glad to spend a night at their ranch. Unfortunately it lost much of its early splendor in the year 1818, when it was plundered by the pirates who were led by Bouchard; but there still remain many of the old houses, interesting in their passing glory.

The Spanish-Californians were distinctly a pastoral people, and many other beautiful and interesting ranches of more recent patent were granted and located throughout the county. Raising cattle for their hides was for many years the principal industry; and the free life of the ranch accorded with the nature-loving spirit of the people.

The busy season at the ranches was in the early summer, when the cattle were rounded up and branded. It was one of the most beautiful times of the year. The last rains had left the grass green, and the fields were still covered with wild flowers. The days were growing longer and the warm sun brightened the land. There was no sound of modern industry or ambition's strife. Only the singing of birds or the lowing of cattle awoke the stillness. It was a dreamland of peace.

Then the owner of the ranch would leave the pueblo with all his family and go to his country home. Work began at early dawn and lasted till sundown, but it was a work that all enjoyed; and when the day's work was done and the sun had set, the families gathered in the open air to listen to the guitar and the songs they loved so dearly. There were light feet and light hearts in the old California days and joyful songs and merry peals of laughter.

The typical ranch life of the early days has passed away, and only a few of the old rancheros remain. Not long ago, one of them was speaking of the ranch where he lived when a boy. "It lay beyond the mountain range," he said, "and extended over rolling hills and little valleys. A creek flowed through it, and on the banks were many sycamores. Shaded by the oaks was the long, low adobe house with its red tiled roof and wide veranda. Behind the fence of chaparral was the orchard and the melon patch, and beyond the orchard was the meadow, golden with buttercups in early spring. In the open fields, dotted with oaks, the rich alfilerilla grew, and on the hillsides were the wild grasses, which waved like billows as the cool breezes from the distant ocean blew over them. The sameness of recurring events of each succeeding year never seemed monotonous, but brought repose, content and peace. When the dew was still on the grass, we would mount our horses and herd the cattle, if any had strayed beyond the pasture In the wooded canyons where the cool brooks flowed, and where the wild blackberries grew, we ate our noonday meal and rested. And as the hills began to glow with the light of the setting sun we sauntered homeward. When the long days of summer came, we ate our evening meals beneath the oaks, and in the twilight we listened to the guitar and the songs of our people. In the autumn we harvested the corn and gathered the olives and grapes.

"Those were days of long ago. Now all is changed by modern progress; but in the simple ranch life of the olden time there as a contented happiness which an alien race with different sentiments and different temperament can never understand.

APPENDIX I.

THE following are the names of all the soldiers, not including the Indian auxiliaries, who were present at the founding of the presidio, and who were known as *soldados de cuera,* on account of the leather jackets which they wore. Many of their descendants became well known in the subsequent life of Santa Barbara.

Captain, Jose Francisco Ortega.
First Lieutenant, Pablo Cota.
Second Lieutenant, Dario Arguello.
First Sergeant, Jose Carrillo.
Second Sergeant, Jose Maria Ortega.
Third Sergeant, Ignacio Olivera.
First Corporal, Pedro Amador.
Second Corporal, Jose Ignacio Rodriquez.

Private Soldiers:

Jose Ayala,	Juan Leyva,	Eugenio Ruiz,
Juan Ballesteros,	Juan Jose Lobo,	Jose Ruiz,
Salvador Cervantes,	Jose Logo,	Tadeo Sanchez,
Mariano Cota,	Luis Logo,	Guillermo Soto,
Juan Dominguez,	Manuel Machado,	Juan Franco Soto,
Anastasio Felix,	Jose I. Martinez,	Eugenio Valdez,
Rosalino Fernandez,	Luis Pena,	Jose Valdez,
Jose M. Flores,	Vicente Quijada,	Juan Valencia,
Francisco Garcia,	Martin Reyes,	Manuel Valenzuela,
Isidro German,	Ignacio Rochin,	Jose Valenzuela,
Felipe Gonzalez,	Joaquin Rodriguez,	Juan Villa,
Tomas Gonzalez,	Juan M. Romero,	Vicente F. Villa.

APPENDIX II.

DERIVATION OF THE NAMES OF LOCALITIES NEAR SANTA BARBARA

Rincon—Is the Spanish equivalent for a Corner, and is applied to the mountain in the northwest corner of Ventura County.

Carpinteria—Is the Spanish equivalent for a Carpenter Shop. The reason for the application of this word to the valley is uncertain. It has been stated that a carpenter shop, *carpinteria,* existed in the valley very many years ago; and that the valley received its name from that circumstance. It has also been stated that when the padres first visited the valley the Indians were engaged as carpenters, building boats; and from this circumstance the valley was named.

Montecito—Is the Spanish equivalent for a Little Wood; and the valley was so named on account of the many groves of trees which grew there.

Mesa—Is the Spanish equivalent for Table, and refers to the table-land along the coast.

Goleta—Is the Spanish equivalent for Schooner. When Captain De la Guerra was sent to Mexico, as habilitado general of California, he took with him a portable writing desk containing a secret drawer, within which were concealed several thousand pesos. Mexico was then in the throes of one of its many revolutions; and as a partisan of the government he was arrested and his private papers removed; but the secret drawer and its contents were undiscovered. Shortly afterwards he made his escape, and with the pesos which he had concealed during his confinement he purchased a schooner, in which he sailed from Mexico and landed at Goleta. That locality was thereafter designated Goleta, with reference to his schooner.

La Patera—Signifies in Spanish a place where ducks congregate; and that locality was so designated on account of the large flocks of wild ducks which formerly frequented the low lands there.

Dos Pueblos—Is the Spanish equivalent for Two Villages; and refers to the two Indian rancherias, one of which was on each side of the creek of that name.

Tecolote—Is the Indian word for An Owl.

Gaviota—Signifies in Spanish a Sea Gull, and that locality was so named from the circumstance, that when Governor Portola and Sergeant Ortega were marching up the coast to found the Mission of Monterey, one of the soldiers shot a sea gull at that locality.

Santa Cruz—Is the Spanish equivalent for Holy Cross. See page 28 for origin of the appellation.

Anacapa—Is an Indian word implying deception in appearance; and was applied to the island on account of the frequent mirages which give it a weird and distorted appearance.

APPENDIX III.

THE DERIVATION OF THE NAMES OF THE STREETS OF SANTA BARBARA
ARE AS FOLLOWS:

Alamar—Is the Spanish for a Grove of Cotton Trees.

Alisos—Is the Spanish for Sycamores, many of which once grew on the street so named.

Anacapa—Is so named because the street points in the direction of the Island of that name. See above.

Anapamu—Is derived from the name of an Indian Chief who ruled over many tribes, principally south of the City of Santa Barbara.

Arrellaga—Is named after Jose Joaquin de Arrellaga, who was governor of California from 1792 to 1794.

Banos—Is the Spanish word for Baths, and the street was so named as it led to that part of the beach where the people generally bathed.

Cacique—Was the title which was applied to the chief of an Indian tribe.

Canal—Is the Spanish for Channel, and the street is said to have been so named because it led to the channel of Santa Barbara.

Carpinteria—Was named after the valley of that name, and was one of the principal thoroughfares leading in that direction. See page 100.

Carrillo—Was named after the Carrillo family, of whom Raimundo

Carrillo was comandante, and Joaquin Carrillo was district judge.

Castillo—Is the Spanish word for Castle or Fort, and the street was so named as it led to the old Spanish fort on the Mesa.

Chapala—Was named by some of the early settlers after the town in Mexico from which they came.

Chino—Was named after the Rancho del Chino, where occurred the battle of San Pascual.

Cota—Was named after the Cota family, one of whom was first lieutenant under Captain Ortega.

Canada—Signifies in Spanish a Ravine, and the street was so named as it extended to a ravine.

Canon Perdido—Derives its name from the following incident: At the time that the regiment of Col. J. D. Stevenson was here, a brass twelve-pound cannon was landed on the beach; but a number of native Californians carried it off at night and hid it in the vicinity of Canon Perdido street. As Canon Perdido is the Spanish equivalent for "lost cannon," the street near where it was buried therafter received that name.

De la Guerra—Was named after the family of that name.

De la Vina—Once called Vineyard street, derived its name from the fact that Comandante Goycoechea owned a vineyard through which the street passed.

Figueroa—Was named after Governor Figueroa, who was governor of Alta California in 1833.

Garden of Jardines—Street if extended would pass through the gardens which in early days were known as the De la Guerra gardens, from which fact the street was so named.

Gillespie—Was named after Captain Gillespie, who had charge of the American troops at the battle of San Pascual.

Gutierrez—Was named after the Guttierez family, who were prominent residents here and in other parts of California. Col. Nicolas Gutierrez was acting governor and military commander of Alta California after Governor Chico.

Haley—Was named after Salisbury Haley, who made what is known in Santa Barbara as the Haley survey.

Indio Muerto—Signifies in Spanish, A Dead Indian, and the street was so named because a dead Indian was found in the locality where the street passes.

Islay—Is the Indian name for the wild cherry which grows on the Santa Ynez Mountains.

Junipero—Is named after Junipero Serra.

Ladera—Is the Spanish word for Declivity, and the street is so named as it is on the hillside.

Laguna—Street extended to the lake or *languna* which existed in early days in the lower part of the city, from which circumstance the name was derived.

Los Olivos—Is the Spanish for Olives; and the street is so named as it passed through the old garden of the Mission where many olive trees grew, and many of which are still standing.

Mason—Was named after Governor Mason, who levied a tax of five hundred dollars to pay for the lost cannon.

Micheltorena—Was named after Manuel Micheltorena, who was appointed governor of Alta California in 1842.

Milpas—Is derived from an Indian word meaning a patch of ground sown to grain. In the early days, large quantities of corn and grain were raised in the vicinity of Milpas street.

Montecito—Street led toward the valley of Montecito, which in Spanish signifies A Little Wood.

Nopal—Is the Indian word for the Prickley Pear.

Pedregosa—Is the Spanish adjective for Stony; and the street was so named after the arroyo Pedregosa which crosses part of it.

Pitos—Is the Spanish word for Flutes, and the street derived its name from the reeds which grew where the street now passes, and from which flutes were made by the Indians.

Pueblo—Signifies in Spanish a Town or Village, and refers to the Indian pueblo near the Mission, which was in the vicinity of that street.

Punta Gorda—Signifies in Spanish a High Bluff, and refers to the bank to which the street extends.

Quaratino—Derived its named from the fact that some ships were once put in quarantine near where the street reaches the beach.

Quinientos—Is the Spanish word for Five Hundred, and the derivation of the name of the street is as follows: The native Californians who had stolen the cannon above referred to alleged that it had been lost by the sailors, in their attempt to place it on the ship which was to convey it to Monterey; but as Governor Mason, to whom the matter was referred, refused to credit the report, he levied a tax of five hundred dollars on the town of Santa Barbara, and a company of soldiers was sent from Los Angeles to force payment. As many of the innocent residents regarded the tax as unwarranted, they refused to pay it, whereupon a sufficient amount of their property was sold to meet their share of the tax.

Rancheria—Was so named on account of a rancheria or Indian village which formely existed in that vicinity.

Robbins—Was named after Captain Thomas M. Robbins, who came to Santa Barbara before 1830, and who formerly owned a ranch to which that street extended.

Salinas—Signifies in Spanish a Salt Marsh, and the street was so named as it extended to a salt pond or marsh.

Salsipuedas—In Spanish (Sal si puedas) means "get out if you can," and the name was applied to the street on account of the many gulches it crossed.

San Andres—Is said to have been named after the location where a revolutionary skirmish occurred between the native Californians.

San Buenaventura—Was named after the pueblo of San Buenaventura, and in Spanish signifies Welcome.

San Pascual—Was named after the battle of San Pascual, which occurred in 1846, between the American forces and the Californians.

Sola—Was named after Vicente de Sola, who was governor of Alta California from 1815 to 1823.

Soledad—Signifies in Spanish, Solitude, and the street was so named because it passed through that part of the town in which there were few inhabintants.

Valerio—Was named after an Indian, who escaped from the Mission about the year 1826, and turned robber. He lived in a cave in the Santa Ynez Mountains, where he hid his spoil.

Victoria—Was named after Manuel Victoria, who was governor of
   Alta California in 1831.
Voluntario—Is the Spanish for Volunteers, and it is stated that Fremont's camp of volunteers was on a hill to which the street
   extended.

Printed in the United States
1020100001B/250